Coping With Transition

Coping With Transition

Men, Motherhood, Money, and Magic

Memoirs from the Lives of
Professional Women

Edited by Susan Briggs Wright

Texas Review Press
Huntsville, Texas

FIRST EDITION, 2011
Requests for permission to reproduce material from this work should
be sent to:

    Permissions
    Texas Review Press
    English Department
    Sam Houston State University
    Huntsville, TX 77341-2146

Cover design by Barnet Levinson
Photograph by Laurie Perez

Library of Congress Cataloging-in-Publication Data

Coping with transition : men, motherhood, money, and magic : memoirs from the lives of professional women / edited by Susan Briggs
Wright. -- 1st ed.
   p. cm.
 ISBN 978-1-933896-78-6 (pbk. : alk. paper)
 1. Autobiography--Women authors. 2. Women in the professions-
-Texas--Houston--Biography. 3. Middle-aged women--Texas--Hous-
ton--Biography. 4. Women employees--Texas--Houston--Biography.
5. Employees--Texas--Houston--Biography. 6. Life cycle, Human-
-Psychological aspects. 7. Maturation (Psychology) 8. Adjustment
(Psychology) I. Wright, Susan Briggs, 1942-
 CT3262.T4C67 2011
 970.72--dc23
 [B]
                        2011024820

To
The Women
of
The Transition Network

The only gift is
a portion of thyself

—Ralph Waldo Emerson

Contents

AUTHOR BIOGRAPHIES

 **Lisa Hankamer**'s love of travel and her success in the hospitality industry have taken her to thirty-eight countries since graduating with a business degree from University of Mississippi. Specializing in capital markets and transactions with the CB Richard Ellis Hotels Group, she enjoys cooking, fishing, writing, and good conversation.

 **Suzanne Kerr**, retired attorney, was a founder and president of the Houston chapter of Women in Commercial Real Estate. Suzanne is currently writing short memoirs, seeking a fresh purpose for the second half of her life, and exploring give-back opportunities. She loves the written word and all things arty.

 **Dorothy Greenberg** is a business leader specializing in human resources management. She earned a graduate degree in applied psychology from Stevens Institute of Technology and a BA in Psychology from Seton Hall University. She's enjoying life in Houston, Texas with her husband, Harvey, and their two canine companions, Sophie and Ivy.

 **Jane Williams** is a divorced attorney living in Houston in a house overrun with dogs, cats and kids. She chauffeurs, tutors, nurses, chefs, volunteers, trampolines, swims, is a pretty good musician and artist, and is weirdly hooked on American Idol. She routinely embarrasses her children, and she is good at it.

 **Mary Margaret Hansen** is a visual artist and writer, inveterate blogger and longtime Houstonian with an Aruban girlhood. She invariably finds herself at the intersection of public service and creative endeavor and is happiest when the two merge. She is at work as civic art consultant for a City of Houston building project.

Susan Lieberman co-founded the Houston TTN chapter. She is the author of six books, the most recent being *The Mother-in-Law's Manual,* and a partner in Y Collaborative (www.ycollaborative.com) that focuses on helping people of all ages put life in order for end of life issues.

Donna Siegel is a writer, a photographer, and admits to an addiction to Photoshop. She holds a bachelor's degree in industrial photography and a master's degree in public health. She has three children and three grandchildren. "Crossing the Rubicon" is adapted from her book, *On the Doorposts of All Our Houses (and what went on inside).*

Sandy Wotiz, retired attorney, chaired the Houston Bar Association's Dispute Resolution Committee and worked on Houston's Special Olympics. This is Sandy's first memoir writing adventure and she is exploring various options to enrich Part Two of her life. She loves music, reading and walking on the beach.

Kristie Husmann is a native of Tulsa, Oklahoma where she won the Miss Tulsa pageant. A Houstonian since age 21, she remains in love with the city and hopelessly smitten with her husband Gary. Other enthusiasms include political community organizing, her German and Cherokee ancestry, and hosting great dinner parties.

Leslie McManis has consulted for clients ranging from small businesses to publicly traded companies and led college courses on negotiations. Her background includes operations management, technology and new and emerging products for banking and finance. She lives near her longtime boyfriend in The Woodlands, and enjoys mystery novels, Jazzercise and seeing friends.

Mel Gallagher was raised in a large family in Washington, D.C. and moved to Texas after marrying in the mid seventies. She worked in the fields of education, politics and public affairs before retiring in Houston. She and her husband have three sons, two daughters-in-law and one grandson.

Sue Jacobson is a vice president with a national firm providing title insurance for commercial real estate. She has served on many non-profit boards and has a passion for great conversation, traveling to interesting countries and meeting extraordinary people. She is particularly fond of Africa, where her mind was freed to develop her interest in writing.

The many faces of **Madeleine G. Appel** include wife, mother, grandmother, friend, journalist, volunteer and government administrator. Currently she serves as Deputy Chief of Staff for the Mayor of Houston. She spends her leisure time curled up with a good mystery, needlepointing or campaigning for her boss.

Thelma Zirkelbach is a speech pathologist and writer of romance novels and creative nonfiction. Having transitioned from wife to widow, she now leads resource classes for others who are going it alone. She loves reading, learning new things and travelling just about anywhere including Antarctica. Her blog is at www.widowsphere.blogspot.com.

Susan Briggs Wright's career has evolved from broadcast journalism to public relations and corporate communications, all useful to her present focus on memoir and family history. She teaches at the Women's Institute of Houston, conducts workshops, and guides individual clients' stories to print and video. Her website is www.memoircoach.com.

Introduction

This book began with the formation of a special interest group on memoir writing within the Houston chapter of The Transition Network (TTN). TTN is a national organization for women over fifty with fifteen chapters around the country. We quickly agreed on the obvious theme and then, with each other's support and input, we wrote about our transition journeys and the insights we've gained. These turned out to cluster around four "M" words: men, motherhood, money, and magic.

Men: Because like the mountains, they're there. And their impact is huge. The fathers who shaped our self-concepts as well as our hopes and fears. Mentors and rivals reacting to our arrival on their turf. The impossible boss, the obnoxious lecher, the considerate first lover, the unfaithful husband, the life partners we choose to share our time and space. The absent men, departed in death or divorce.
Motherhood: Because in our era, it became an option.
Money: Because we widened our horizons and gained more.
Magic: Because it covers not only our science and technology, but also intuition and spirituality that we barely understand. And it starts with *M*.

We were born between 1935 and 1960. The strong common thread in our lives is our emphasis on career and self-development. But where culture is concerned, the oldest and youngest of us came of age in different worlds. In 1953, Hollywood brought out *How To Marry a Millionaire*, with Marilyn Monroe, Betty Grable and Lauren Bacall—glamour girls on a manhunt for wealthy prey. In real life, achieving the "M-R-S degree" by college graduation was more important than finding the highest and best use of a woman's talents. Three pink career lanes were promoted en route to the altar: nursing (How to Marry a Doctor), secretarial work (How to Marry the Boss) and teaching (Something to Fall Back On). Memoirs from women who departed from these traditional roles show the difficult challenges they found in their passages.

By the time the youngest among us went to work, the triple-threat Hollywood comedy team was Dolly Parton, Lily Tomlin and Jane Fonda ganging up on their boss from hell. In real life, many women were choosing careers like men had always done—with a focus on money and status. Many of us adapted our plumage according to the data-driven teachings of *Dress For Success*. But you can almost hear the *9 to 5* theme throbbing as background music for recollections of condescension, harassment, and simple, categorical exclusion.

The Pill did not eliminate painful issues around the motherhood option. What happens when spouses can't agree about having children? Will a challenging international adoption create a fulfilling family for a single divorcee—or a disaster? How stressful is the competition between a young family and tough law school exams? How does a writer preserve her professional identity when she leaves Madison Avenue for a mommy track in dusty and snowy outposts far from New York?

We joke that we are becoming our mothers and grandmothers, but that is far from true. Many of them never reached the age we have attained. Some were overwhelmed by large families, marital difficulties, and mental health issues. We have been blessed with our access to education, our medical and pharmaceutical sciences, contact lenses, and cosmetology. We have media and technology that bring the globe to our digital devices, powerful demographics, and a zeitgeist that encourages us to keep growing. Two real estate professionals on a lark in Northern Italy—*Perfetto*! A rekindled romance at sixty-eight—Expect the unexpected! A seventy-nine-year-old writer "addicted" to Photoshop brings out her own book—High fives and fist bumps! But how can we fail to see the reality of the lovers' aging, or the edginess of the city hall insider contemplating retirement? Or forget the sobs of the wife about to become a widow? On good days, this time of life seems like a ride in the surrey with the fringe on top: *Don't you wish it would go on forever—don't you wish it'd go on forever—and never stop—?*

It won't go on forever. So we recall and share the transitions of our lives to date—watching, learning, and coping.

Susan Briggs Wright
Houston, 2011

Coping With Transition

Men, Motherhood, Money, and Magic

Menopaulic Magnolia

Lisa Hankamer

Menopaulic Magnolia

Lisa Hankamer

May 2010 Jackson, Mississippi—Airport Bar—flight delayed

Hello, my name is Lisa. I am an original magnolia from Mississippi. I turn fifty-one this weekend and I'm a Menopaulic. This is very difficult for me. We don't talk about things like this down in the Deep South. I've been pursuing denial for over a year now and seeking recovery.

I look pretty good for my age, keeping myself together thanks to Jose, my soulful facialist, and a fabulous hair colorist who keeps the grey in check. It's my body that has me worried—this shell of mine which is morphing into an indefinable shape. And I absolutely refuse to use today's standard, patronizing response, "Turning into an apple shape happens to everyone your age—it's inevitable." What a bunch of sage bullshit! However, I am not in panic mode. I just need to derail this MF process as soon as possible.

Therefore, I am pursuing the steps for recovery. A visit to the endocrinologist confirmed that I am ragingly hormonal with numbers for the bad stuff way past the normal range. Got the prescriptions. My assistant just presented me with the book, *Eating for a Hormonally Healthful Life*. I think she's really worried about me. And, for the first time, I've consulted with a spiritual advisor. She read my palm, gave me some special bracelets to create calm, and prepared a secret parfumetic potion which I am to apply in an intimate place in order to attract the right people into my life. Has anyone really heard of Black Cohosh and is it legal?

Thank God for girlfriends. And red wine. And girl talk.

As we attempt to create clarity out of this life process, what we actually find is that we are perpetually operating within a state of fuzziness. We are so accustomed to being in charge—of our lives, our families, our relationships, our finances, our hopes, our dreams—it's an aura of independence we, as women, have created all by ourselves. We've had goals. We've been producers. We've been successful. We've been orgasmic. We have had purpose and direction. We have given direction. We have given time. We have given money. We have overcome. We've even received minimal recognition for our good works and deeds.

And yet, here I am, along with many other Sisters in this incredible state of fuzziness. The picture going forward is foggy; the directions to pursue are not clear-cut; the decisions to make are put off, as if, for the first time, we are unsure.

Intelligently, we locate our support groups who help to empower us through this life-change transition. We look for spiritual guidance, immerse ourselves in yoga, boot camp, or plastic surgery as an escape. And yet, there is still no clear course leading us to the other side. Where is the 12-Step Plan for menopausal recovery and who has hidden it?

I want passion back in my life. I do not wish to be just content. I do not wish to be accepting. I do not wish to call attention to my current hormonal state or use it as an excuse. I do know that I would not go back, but am unsure of how to go forward. Now there seems to be a time limit in place for all the things I want to do "When I grow Up" and "When I have the Time." It's new to me, this press of time, and I fear not making the best of it. It's all just so fuzzy.

However, I'm the proverbial optimist and I know that this too shall pass. The dual personality of my Gemini birthright is just stuck on the downside and something will eventually shake it loose. Maybe it is really not so depressing that we get to experience this journey. Could it be that the M phase is truly a special gift?

Perhaps we require this major hormonal upheaval as a sign to stop and take stock. To make us question the current life path, and encourage us to find new ones to pursue. Maybe we need to get all shook up in order to get our body's natural rhythms back into place. This place of fuzzy could be our coping mechanism, providing us with a time-out for reconfiguring our futures. For determining new directions. For moving to new music. What a thought.

It's time to hike up my Spanx and move forward, confident in the fact that I will come out on the other side with a new sense of purpose. There will be new friends and faces there, welcoming me with open arms. And, there will be no fuzzy. And, there will be no fear—simply a childlike eagerness for life's next pursuit.

Until my awakening presents itself, I'll just get comfortable with my fuzziness, allowing it to humor me. What else can you do but laugh? Or cry. Or see your shrink. Or get laid. Or take a pill. Or try that new Zumba class. Wait! My flight is finally being called! How appropriate! How enlightening! Grabbing my baggage, I realize what it's all about. I am simply operating as a delayed airplane flight—as a result of extreme turbulence—soon to be rerouted in order to continue the Journey. Now I get it and no sweat! Wonder if I'll be awarded double frequent flier miles for this one?

See ya on the other side. MM

Waiting For Marriage, Sex and My Mother's Life (In That Order)

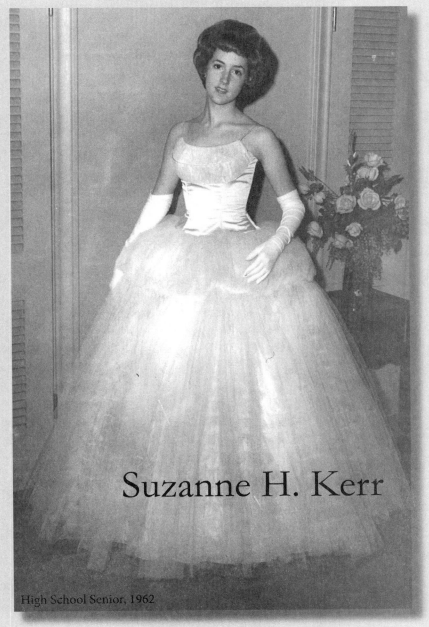

High School Senior, 1962

Suzanne H. Kerr

With family at sister's wedding, 1971

Kaye Marvins Photography

In therapy, 1978

Our wedding, 1988

Costumed as Julia and Paul Child, 2010

Waiting for Marriage, Sex and My Mother's Life (In That Order)

Suzanne H. Kerr

I grew up in Victoria, Texas, a two-hour drive from Houston. My attorney father thought it important to be above reproach at all times. He expected his girls to be virtuous young women who would never be "talked about." Our family's reputation in the town where he was born meant everything to him. My father was strict about who I could go out with and where I could go. He was never really happy with anyone I dated unless he knew the boy's parents. Problem was—hardly any of my parents' friends had boys my age, and my closest friends had only sisters or much younger brothers. A lot of things were off-limits for me: drive-in movies ("that's where girls go to meet boys their fathers won't let them date"), off-campus pep rallies ("things might get out of hand"), unchaperoned parties ("never a good idea"), the public swimming pool ("you have the pool at the country club"), etc. My mother was in full agreement with my father on these matters (she was from a family of girls). Even if she had, on occasion, privately disagreed, she would never have contradicted him. My mother put my father first, her children second, her community activities third, and herself last. So, as the elder of two daughters, I was successfully trained by two very nice, well-intentioned people to respect authority, follow rules, avoid risk, and care about what other people thought of me. I wanted to meet everyone's expectations of me, and I wanted everyone to like me.

September 1962 I sat on the front porch steps with my father. He wanted to have a word with me before I left for college. He was serious and chose his words carefully: "Suzy, the next four years will be the most carefree time of your entire life. You will be able to learn, grow and generally enjoy yourself, so I urge you to make the most of it. I don't care what you major in so long as you get a teaching certificate in case you ever have to work. Once you've graduated, you'll be off the payroll. If you marry before you graduate, you'll be off the payroll. And, Suzy, don't plan to return to Victoria. There's really nothing here for you. Choose a large city like Houston or Dallas. I would advise you not to drink or smoke, and if I ever hear that you've gone to a boy's apartment, I'll jerk you out of school." My mother, bless her heart, had already conveyed similar, but more personal messages: "Your father and I agree that you must be a virgin when you marry. The kind of man you would want to marry would expect a virgin—and he would know if you were not. We also agree that you should marry a professional man."

I understood the "graduate before you marry" part and "there's nothing for you in Victoria" part. Daddy already knew I smoked because I had whipped out a Salem during an argument to irritate him. The drinking part was only cautionary because both of my parents were social drinkers. But for God's sake, what was going to happen to me if I went to a boy's apartment? Was the boy going to turn into an unbridled animal and have his way with me? And how in the world would a man know if I was or was not a virgin?

Suffice it to say that during my college years I was a terrible date. I didn't know how to relate to boys—which meant I didn't know how to make them feel comfortable—which meant that second and third dates with the same guy were hard to come by. I was the prototypical prude in all respects, but I was always dreaming of romance. My mother had told me that sex would be beautiful in marriage, but not before. I was looking forward to living my girlhood dream of falling in love, getting married, having sex, having babies, and volunteering in the community—in that order. When the U.S. and Russia went toe to toe during the Cuban Missile Crisis in the fall of 1962, the girls in my dorm were calling their parents and boyfriends. Not me. I was calling God: "You can't let me die a virgin! It just wouldn't be fair!"

June 1966 Days after graduating from college with the fail-safe teaching certificate in hand, my friend, Susan, and I flew to Europe. We planned to work and travel for a year. We were both still "intact" and frequently joked about how we would handle European men who would no doubt expect sex. As it turned out, we rarely dated any European men because all of our contacts were Americans in the military. Even though I was far from home and "the rules," I only progressed to "petting"—which was waist up and fully clothed. Waist down was off limits; our girdles protected us from second thoughts when things heated up. One evening after a date, I told Susan I thought something was wrong with me because my panties and girdle were soaking wet. Susan screamed with laughter and explained to me what "getting excited" can do to your body. She had an older sister, so she knew a thing or two.

Two months into our European adventure, Susan met Mike, an engineer from North Carolina doing a four-year stint in the army. They fell in love before my very eyes, and it was thrilling to watch their relationship unfold in just the right way. Four months later, Susan and I returned to the States (still "intact") to prepare for her wedding. Susan and Mike married in February 1967 and returned to Europe to complete his tour of duty. Two weeks later, another dear friend married and moved to Tulsa. I was a bridesmaid in both weddings. At the conclusion of the second, my father asked me: "When will I be walking you down the aisle?" He was just being a dad, but the question really bothered me. I had no prospects and he knew it. To make matters worse, I was moving to Houston where I had friends, but not best friends. The thought of starting a new life there was depressing; my heart wasn't in it. Six memorable months of living, working, and traveling in Europe had spoiled me.

1967-1969 In Houston, I taught high school English and lived with two friends at the Chateaux Dijon Apartments. We had a two-bedroom apartment in the three-story "castle" section—one of the "in" places to live at that time. All of our furnishings were hand-me-downs from our parents. We refused to buy new furniture or accessories because we viewed that as a sign we would be old maids. We tried to look nice at all times because our raison d'être was to find a man, get married, and stop working as soon as possible.

Most of our mothers had never worked for pay; they had been community volunteers. As one of my friends put it, "I can't help it, I was raised to be a liability." Unfortunately, there were several obstacles in our way. We couldn't go anywhere in the evenings without a date—not to movies, theaters, or restaurants—except perhaps on Sunday night. The Sunday night exception was a carryover from our college days when the dorms and sorority houses didn't serve meals on Sunday nights. Sometimes, if we found ourselves dateless on Saturday night, we closed our curtains, turned out all of the lights, and ate in the dark. That way no one knew we were at home. If we hadn't had an opportunity to dress up in a long time, we prepared a nice dinner for ourselves and ate in our cocktail dresses. We were determined to make the best of it. We spent our spare time at the various pools in the complex trying to look adorable. Mostly we were ignored because the guys were too busy playing water volleyball. I wasn't getting anywhere.

After two years of teaching school during the day (primarily with women) and twiddling my thumbs in the evening, I decided to move to greener pastures. I had worked in Washington, D.C. as a summer intern during college. The entire experience was magical—made more so because one of my friends worked at the White House. D.C. was crawling with young men and women who were smart and interesting and serious of purpose—just the way I wanted to be. My attraction to D.C. was renewed when I drove down to Victoria for the wedding of an old friend. The bride worked for Senator John Tower of Texas; the groom worked for Senator Howard Baker of Tennessee. Their D.C. friends—all attractive and engaging—raved about life in D.C. and assured me I would have no trouble finding a good job there. After her honeymoon, the bride lined me up with roommates and a job interview. So, I packed myself up, waved goodbye to my bewildered family and friends, and drove to D.C. in an old Chevrolet crammed with everything I owned.

1969-1970 Washington, D.C. turned out to be just what the doctor ordered. Women could go anywhere at any time, and no one thought a thing about it. Most parties were wide open—which meant that no one brought dates because you wanted to meet as many of the opposite sex as you could. It felt like being free to BE—like it felt when we started doing the twist in college and girls could do their own thing rather than having to follow the boy's lead. It was exhilarating. Not only that, but women held responsible jobs and were going to graduate school in droves. I was in awe of the entire scene. I started dating more and found that the kind of men D.C. attracted were far more interesting to me than the Houston boys I'd left behind. It was easy to find people who shared my views.

Of course, sex was still a sticking point for me, but help was on the way. I discovered that women, even the very nicest Southern girls who had attended Sweetbriar, Smith, and the like, discussed sex openly, and I was all ears. They didn't discuss details—a la *Sex and the City*—but the mere fact that sex was being discussed at all was helpful. However, when Carol told us matter-of-factly, "I always carry my diaphragm with me on dates, just in case," we were dumbfounded. It implied that Carol might consider sex on the *first* date. I had only recently gotten past the "don't kiss on the first date" rule. You can best believe I thought a lot about that. Some of these women—in more private settings—were even talking about orgasms and masturbation. It was just a matter of time before I finally gave myself permission to have sex for the very first time.

I was almost twenty-seven and had fallen head over heels in love with John. The "in love" state of being was nothing short of miraculous to me. I wanted to give up my virginity to John even though I knew in my heart I wasn't the one for him. John was a Jewish intellectual from Boston who was attending law school at Berkeley. He wanted to be a labor arbitrator. He viewed life as a series of obstacles to be overcome. I, on the other hand, was a WASP sorority girl from Texas who wanted to get married, quit work, and have babies. I looked at the world through rose-colored glasses, so I couldn't see the great divide between us. John was surprised to learn that I was a virgin, and he wasn't sure he wanted to be my first. However, months later, lust won out and it was wonderful. I had chosen a very tender and sensitive young man to usher me into womanhood. The next morning, as I was brushing my hair in front of the mirror, he asked me, "How did you like it?" All I could do was blush and smile and nod.

WAITING FOR MARRIAGE AND MY MOTHER'S LIFE

1971–1972 Following the huge, beautiful sexual breakthrough, I soon had to accept the fact that John was not in it for the long haul. He had never led me to think otherwise, but I kept hoping he would fall for me the way I had fallen for him. Our relationship slowly morphed into a friendship, and the hole in my heart healed. I was now a twenty-seven-year-old woman with no marriage prospects. However, I had learned that the kind of man I wanted to marry would be grateful that I was *not* a virgin! My feeling of optimism about my future was heightened by the marriage of my twenty-three-year-old sister to a wonderful young man from Houston with a fine education and a good heart.

My mother told me, on more than one occasion, that before she met my father, she was afraid she'd be an old maid. She met my father at twenty-three and married him at twenty-four. The old maid stigma was very threatening to me because a husband was the ticket to the only life I had ever envisioned for myself. I no doubt started worrying about marriage when I was in high school. I wrote my career day paper on being a housewife and mother (the remuneration was pride, love, etc.). My yearbook bore such remarks as: "Don't marry the first one that comes along," and "I hope you get a Texan!" Because I didn't find the right man until I was forty-three, I slogged around in the singles world for too many years to count. Many of the relationships along the way brought heartbreak because I was simply trying too hard.

I next fell in love with a seriously talented and very nice young attorney who had been separated from his wife for a few months. He had had cancer and become sterile, and his wife had reacted as though she were the victim—shunning him during his treatment and later leaving him. I thought I was safe. However, when his wife learned he was interested in someone else, she begged him to give the marriage a second chance. He was gone in a flash. He told me he was sorry, but that didn't assuage the shock and heartache. How could I have been so foolish?

I much too quickly got involved with yet another attorney who had come to D.C. to work for the IRS. He was not everything I had hoped for in a man, but I was so desperate to get married that I would have said yes had he proposed. His commitment to the government would be up in a year, so time was on my side—or so I thought. When eight months had passed, he started talking about the future, but his plans did not appear to include me. Initially, I thought he was trying to gauge my reaction to his plans, so I enthusiastically endorsed all of his ideas, including his desire to practice law in San Francisco. As time passed, however, there was no hint of commitment and I began to slowly implode. He was not the least sympathetic to my feelings—which made things even worse. As I became more and more nervous, clingy and teary, he became detached and even callous about it. The relationship crashed and burned, and I was left a bewildered, nervous wreck with a gnawing pain in my stomach.

1973–1975 I returned to Houston to recover—not realizing that I couldn't run from the emotional turmoil I was experiencing. Three failed relationships in two and a half years had been too much. Moving only made it worse. I woke up each morning, and within seconds, a vice-like grip took hold of my chest. This was exactly how my father had described his condition prior to a breakdown in the early sixties. He recovered and returned to work, but was plagued with periodic bouts of anxiety and depression for the rest of his life. I was terrified that I was headed down the same path, but afraid to discuss it with anyone. My only consolation was remembering what my bright-eyed mother once told me, "I wake up every morning with a little bubble of happiness in my throat." Her genes just had to win out.

The return to Houston was the worst period of my life. I was clinically depressed and trying to tough it out. At the same time, I was dealing with a new job and trying to reach out to old friends. To make matters worse, I soon discovered that Houston hadn't changed much since I'd been gone. Women could do more on their own, but life in general was the same. Most single women I knew were still working at low-paying jobs, fulfilling Junior League requirements, and otherwise looking for husbands. Married women lived in a world apart. A divorced acquaintance spoke the sad truth, "My married friends can't wait for me to remarry so that I can be with them again." Would I ever join that married world? Each day I would return from work, close my apartment door, and cry my eyes out. My mantra became: "I've been happy before; I'll be happy again." Mary Tyler Moore had been my TV friend in my twenties, and now Rhoda was my TV friend. When someone asked Rhoda what it felt like to be engaged, she said, "A little knot deep in my stomach has finally relaxed." After living with my raging knot for a couple of months, I finally went to the doctor. I was diagnosed with ulcer symptoms and properly medicated. It took me six miserable months to shed the anxiety I was experiencing. Little did I know that therapy could have gotten me over the hump much more quickly.

In the summer of 1973, I wrote a poem that compared my single life to the lives of my married friends and even touted some of my advantages. However, I also expressed what I was yearning for:

For the "we" which is mutual and full of possibilities
For the security of care, the "call me when you get
*   there safely"*
For receptivity when the need, urge, joy, desire moves
*   you to touch*
For the bloom of well-being, the lush of contentment
For the occasional humdrum of routine which you fight
*   continually but don't mind so much since it's shared*
For the joy of making each day unique for someone
*   other than self to delight*

For a human soul who agrees that the feelings of all
*   manner of men ought to be respected*
Who cares about his work
Loves learning for learning's sake
For one who gives some thought to the poem you push
*   under his nose, indulges your eccentric friends,*
*   returns your passion and is eager to share children*

In November 1974, Prudence Mackintosh wrote a piece for *Texas Monthly* entitled "Crossing Into Thirty." It was all about married life and children—the life I was supposed to be living. It upset me so much that I wrote a response called "Crossing into Thirty Single"—but I stopped short of sending it in. The disclosure that I was no longer a virgin would have embarrassed by parents. The following excerpt illustrates my despair as I coped with loneliness:

I try to plan something for every third night or so. It means calling around, but that's ok. If people aren't interested in the theater or a concert, just meeting for a drink or dinner and a long conversation can do wonders for the spirit. A single woman has to work at feeling a part of the world out there—she has to believe that they really need her at the office, no matter how routine her job may be; that her married friends are sincere when they say, "Please call us anytime. We're home and would love to see you"; that a man to share love with may be just around the

18

corner; that her life matters to the world even if she isn't reproducing or doing much more than supporting herself. Sometimes it is not that easy to be positive.

Another thing I worry about is emotional stability. If my life is to be a series of short-term relationships with men, rather than one long-term marriage, will I be able to hold my own emotionally throughout? The way our society works, it is much harder for a woman to be single than a man. When a woman dates a man, she is usually drawn into his world—she sees his friends, learns about his business, probably spends more time at his place than at hers—so that if a break occurs, it is the woman who is left to find her bearings again. The trauma of being alone again is one thing, but being cut off from the circle of friends you are used to—and have become attached to—is devastating. His friends will sometimes keep up with you, but rarely. They were his friends first, and they'll keep socializing with him, and that's just the way it is.

1975–1978 Once I recovered physically and emotionally, I looked around and realized that Houston still wasn't my cup of tea. I returned to Washington, D.C. to prove to myself that I could, in fact, make a life for myself there and, of course, find a husband. My family was concerned, but supportive. All they wanted was my happiness. I landed a terrific job with the State of Texas office and took a small apartment situated blocks from The Kennedy Center, George Washington University and my office. Life was good. By this time, I viewed men and sex from a completely different perspective. Before, I had only had sex with men I was in love with and wanted to marry. Now, I decided I could have sex with men I liked, but did not want to marry, simply to satisfy my desire for sex. I felt totally comfortable with the decision.

I was under the impression that I had grown up—that my judgment about relationships with men had improved—but sadly I was wrong. My goal was still that knight in shining armor who would give me the life I was raised to live. It took a disastrous, long-distance relationship with a Belgian to spur the next stage of my development. When his volatile, narcissistic personality surfaced, it scared me to death. That old knot in my stomach reappeared, but this time I was smart and went directly to a therapist.

HOPING, BUT NOT WAITING, FOR MARRIAGE

1978–1982: Therapy is a wonderful thing. I talked through the latest debacle and learned what narcissism really means. I ended the long-distance relationship and started working on understanding why—at thirty-four—I was still single. I told the therapist I felt like damaged goods because I had tried and failed at love so often. Together we covered a lot of territory. The real breakthrough came when I realized that my pattern was subservience to men. I was so anxious to please that I suppressed my own thoughts and feelings and generally went along with whatever men said or wanted to do. If a date suggested a movie, I'd agree even if I'd already seen it and didn't really want to see it again. I avoided conflict like the plague because I thought that arguing would mark the end of a relationship. I had never heard my parents argue. My mother never contradicted my father in my presence. She always went along with whatever he said. She even voted like he did because she "didn't want to cancel out his vote." It finally became clear to me that I had never brought my authentic self to a relationship with a man. How two-dimensional I must have seemed, how boring.

While we worked through my issues, the therapist encouraged me to think about what kind of future I wanted for myself whether or not I ever got married. I knew I wanted to make enough money to give myself a home and a nice lifestyle. Medicine was out, so I thought about accounting and law. Several of my D.C. friends were in graduate school. When my D.C. friend, Ann, told me she was entering law school and would be taking classes at night, I thought she was crazy. Poor Ann, her whole life would be work and school for four long years and she'd still come out with a mountain of debt. Well, that was one day. In the twinkling of an eye, Ann had graduated with honors and was working at a prestigious D.C. law firm making what seemed like huge money to me. So why was I sitting on my hands? My father was a lawyer, my brother-in-law was a lawyer, many of my friends were married to lawyers. What was holding me back? I think I questioned whether I could compete with men at that level.

I studied hard for the LSAT and aced it—which bolstered my courage. When I disclosed my plans to my parents, to my utter amazement, they quickly got on board. My father, who never liked women on the golf course or in the courtroom, was finally accustomed to women lawyers. He had hired one and thought highly of her. I entered the University of Texas School of Law and felt privileged to be there. When I graduated, I joined a firm in Houston. Why Houston? Washington D.C. was an exciting city to live in, but it's a revolving door for politicians, lobbyists, and young people seeking "Washington experience." You need to love the political environment to stay there, and I didn't love it enough. I wanted a more traditional city, closer to my family. By this time, my sister had two children and I loved being with her and her family. Plus, several of my friends had divorced, so I knew there would be women friends to pal around with. Houston finally seemed right.

1983-1989 Returning to Houston as an attorney felt like a victory. I worked night and day, but really loved what I was learning. The money was good, and it was fascinating to see how deals are made and problems solved. I was giving legal advice to men, and men were learning to value my opinion. It mattered not that I was a woman; all they wanted was responsiveness and good work. Marriage was still on my mind, but not front and center. I no longer needed a man for money, and at thirty-nine, my childbearing years were over. What I needed from a man was love, passion, common interests, and a commitment to common goals. I could take my time and get it right. Work was challenging, and there were friends to play and travel with. Several of my divorced friends didn't even want to get married again. I dated several men and one, in particular, still makes me laugh. *Time* magazine came out with an article on women and marriage that said: If a woman has not married by the time she is forty, she is more likely to be shot by a sniper than to get married for the first time. Well, my gentleman friend had a heyday with that one. I found the article depressing, but my absorbing work kept it from getting me down.

People used to tell me, "The right man will come along when you least expect it." So true. I first met David in 1979 in Washington, D.C. He was in love with a friend of mine. We had brief conversations at two parties before I moved back to Texas for law school. Years later, we both ended up working in Houston. When David called me in the fall of 1987, I immediately remembered him. After our second date, we were clearly smitten. When sex came up, he placed that decision

21

entirely in my hands. How novel! If men only knew how well that approach works. I couldn't hold back for long and thus began the first serious relationship I'd had in years.

David worked for Exxon. He had a doctorate in education and was in the process of overhauling Exxon's drilling engineering curriculum. He loved his work. Of course, I immediately began asking myself the usual questions: Why is a man this old still single? Is he normal? What kind of baggage is he carrying from his four-year marriage to his college sweetheart? No doubt he was asking himself similar questions about me. It helped that we had mutual friends in D.C. One couple I respected had chosen David to be the godfather of their second son. That was a good sign. Two months into the romance, I invited my sister, her husband, and an old friend to dinner to meet David. My sister and brother-in-law were favorably impressed as was my friend. In her inimitable style, my friend advised: "Suzy, promise me one thing. Don't move in with him before you get married." David and my parents were a match made in heaven. It helped that he was the son of a Presbyterian minister and had beautiful manners. He wasn't a Texan, but he could talk oil with my father and art with my mother. He was a good man and they knew it, and that was all that mattered. David soon had the Good Housekeeping Seal of Approval from everyone.

David was getting plenty of push-back from me which he said he liked. He always knew what was on my mind; I rarely held anything back. By God, I was going to lay it all out there no matter what the consequence. He needed to know me well and love me anyway. He was concerned I expected high-end everything; I was afraid he was a penny-pincher. That led to some spirited conversations. Christmas came and went. My February birthday came and went, and I started to wonder when he would pop the question. He had talked around it, but never officially asked. Only later did I understand how carefully and painstakingly David makes important decisions. He no doubt had spreadsheets on me. In May of 1988, David proposed while we were walking on the Rice University campus. After I said yes, we returned to his car where champagne was chilling in the trunk. The vintage was 1979—the year we met. After word of our engagement got out, the former gentleman friend called to congratulate me: "I hear you beat the odds!"

David and I were married a year after we had our first date; I was a forty-four-year-old bride! My father walked me down the aisle and I promptly burst into tears at the altar. After years of yearning for matrimony, the emotion could not be checked. I made it through the vows and recovered in time for the kiss. Our guests were thrilled for us. We have a precious picture of my father at the reception—all smiles, arms held high above his head. He was reportedly exclaiming, "Free at last!" He no doubt viewed an unmarried daughter as a contingent liability. So on that happy evening, his Depression-era worries were lightened.

David and I honeymooned in Paris—a lovely start to married life. Our first year together was good, but not without its problems. I kept saying "so far, so good" which would really upset him. Thank God for Chipper, David's golden retriever, who served as a wonderful stress reliever for us.

2010 Now, twenty-two years later, David and I feel as though we've been married forever. We are grateful we found each other and have come to deeply appreciate the old adage: a good marriage is a miracle of time and place. The "we" I envisioned in my lonely poem— "mutual and full of possibilities"—has been realized.

When I retired from work two years ago, I finally started living my mother's life. At ninety-four, she still watercolors; I write. She volunteers at her retirement community; I volunteer in the nonprofit community. She goes to church; I sing in the choir. She plays bridge; I work Sudoku puzzles. We both love art, movies, Mexican food, margaritas and, of course, David. She gives unconditional love to everyone; I'm still working on that.

My Impossible Choice

Portrait by Patrick R. Cox Photography

Wedding Day Hopes and Dreams—September 29, 1991

Dorothy Greenberg

My Impossible Choice

Dorothy Greenberg

Harvey is a strong athletic man with broad shoulders. He has a chiseled ethnic look with olive skin, a full mustache, hazel eyes, and beautiful wavy salt-and-pepper hair that a man of any age would envy. I like to call him my "manly man." He's the epitome of what I think a real man should be. Of course, he loves sports and cars and all things electronic. He's a linear thinker and more intelligent than most. But, he's also quick to smile and has a warm and gregarious personality to match. He is candid, even-tempered, and kind. He's a man of integrity and conviction. But, most attractive to me is his quick wit and never ending, and sometimes silly, sense of humor. I'm incredibly attracted to Harvey in a chemical sort of way. I can barely keep my hands off him and from time to time he has to remind me that we are in public or that the kids will see. He consumes me and I like it. But how do I begin my story?

Let me start with how we came to the "Agreement," our verbal contract and pact. I met Harvey seven-years after the end of his first marriage. At that time, his sons, Todd and Jason, were seventeen and fifteen. Harvey was forty-three and I was twenty-eight. From the start our attraction was very physical, but also much deeper. By the third or fourth date he was my best friend. Because of our age difference we agreed from the beginning that we would only be friends. Fifteen weeks later we were engaged. Even though it defied logic, we knew within a few weeks of our first meeting that we would be together. We knew each other from the start. I was totally at ease with Harvey and more myself with him than I had ever been with any other man. I think he felt this way too. It wasn't because we had so much in common. Somehow from day one, we just "got each other" without ever trying to put the best foot forward. It was a feeling of acceptance and understanding that I'd never had before.

I wasn't used to making major decisions based on feelings and faith. I was the pragmatic, serious, hard-working child of immigrant parents who learned at a very early age that there was no tooth fairy. I had put myself through school waiting tables and earned a graduate degree in psychology. I knew better; but, for the first time in my life I took a very deep breath, and then I led more with my heart than with my head. Somehow, I knew that things would work out. They just had to.

It was on our third date that I found out about the "V," the third party of sorts in our relationship. He didn't want any more children and so when his second son, Jason, was two-years-old, Harvey took steps to ensure it would never again be a concern. Thirteen years later, the "V"—the Vasectomy—would become my enemy. At first I didn't think it would be an obstacle. I wasn't thinking of having children. Being one of nine children—yes, nine, but that's another story—I always said that my mother had her children as well as mine.

Getting married before we knew each other one year was all wrong. He was fifteen years older than I, Jewish, divorced, and had two teenage boys. He had lived an entire life before I met him. I was a Christian and had never been married. Hell, I had never even had the desire to commit to a man. I had never lived with a boyfriend or even dated a man with children. I had a life plan of long-term mo- nogamous relationships. But, somehow, we worked. I had an instant family and I felt like I had found a home. We completed the family by adopting a puppy, an adorable but obstinate female beagle whom we appropriately named Gidget.

I loved the boys from the start, because they were Harvey's sons and honestly just great kids. I came out of nowhere and upset their lives; but, they welcomed me because they love their father and want- ed him to be happy. I'm sure it wasn't easy for them, particularly for Jason, the younger of the two. Whereas, Todd went away to college the month we were married, Jason would live with us for the first two years of our marriage, before we moved to Chicago. After the move, neither of the boys lived with us again. I never tried to be Todd's and Jason's mother; they already had one. But, I very much wanted their respect and love.

The first two years of our marriage were wonderful. Sure, there were a lot of adjustments for all of us, but I was very much in love, in a way in which I had never known before and couldn't have imagined. I earned a promotion at work and my employer relocated Harvey and me from New Jersey to Chicago. We had been living the fairytale; so, how was it possible that we were now on the verge of collapse? Suddenly I understood in a real way, a visceral way, what people mean when they say, "Love is not enough."

I hate it, but it was true for me, loving Harvey also awakened maternal stirrings. I wanted to have his child. That's where the Agreement came into play. As impractical as it may have been, when we agreed to get married we also agreed not to discuss the "baby issue" further for two years. I tried to put the Agreement out of my mind as long as possible, and I more than honored it for two and a half years. I kept pushing it down. But, it eventually bubbled up and rose to the top. It was the worst possible time, as I had just lost my eldest brother. "Lost." What a funny way to put it, as if spending thirty minutes searching would bring the huge relief of having him found. No, he wasn't lost. It was the word that I don't say and lie about at every turn. It was suicide. On Thanksgiving Day, he leapt from an overpass onto a highway. And, the horrible pain of my brother's sudden and violent death made me want a baby even more. I needed someone into whom I could lose myself and pour all of my love and hopes.

The truth is that I had lied to myself and to Harvey. I just didn't know it at the time. I lied that we could figure it out later. I really believed that Harvey would break down and eventually give me a baby someday, somehow. I thought that he would at least try by reversing the dreaded "V." And, if that didn't work, we would adopt a baby girl from China. I thought Harvey would love me so much that he would figure out a way to give me a baby. I thought he would acquiesce. Harvey kept telling me, "It's not because I don't want to give you a baby, it's because I can't. Physically, emotionally, or in any other way." He didn't have the desire or energy to parent a baby all over again. He was pushing fifty. He wouldn't bring another child into the world, especially one that he didn't want. "Oh, my God," I thought, "this isn't how it was supposed to happen!" As if to push it in my face at every turn, we were close friends with another newly married couple, John and Lilly. They were in a very similar situation. But, John reversed his

V, and within a few years they had a beautiful baby boy. Did John love Lilly more than Harvey loved me? Don't the women usually have the last word in these matters?

No one tells you about the impossible decisions and compromises that you may have to make in order to maintain a marriage. You know that a lot of marriages end in divorce, but nothing prepares you for something like this. Is it possible to stay with a man you love with all your being, but who will not have a child with you? It was difficult for me to grasp, but I began to come to terms with the reality of the situation. If I stayed with Harvey, I would have to give up my child, forever. You see, my baby wasn't hypothetical. She was a girl, whom I had already named Rachel. I'd created her face and personality and started to develop a relationship with her. Sometimes I talked to her. I was impatient to hold Rachel and begin our life journey together. I began to hate him for denying me my daughter. I was convinced that if he loved me enough he would find a way to give Rachel to me. But, he was steadfast. In a caring yet unyielding way, he didn't give me what I needed most.

So many people procreate by accident or without a second thought. But Harvey stood by what he knew to be the right thing for him, and as he said, "for a child." He was no longer capable of being a participative father to a small child. He just couldn't do it again. His pain must have been great. Perhaps it broke his heart to deny me, as much as it broke my heart to be denied. But, at that time, I was too self-absorbed in my own needs and pain to know. My anger with Harvey was intensified by my passion for him. As they say, "two sides of the same coin." But, now the decision was mine and Harvey was at the mercy of it. Would I stay with him? Or, would I leave him with the hope of one day having my daughter? Thus began the real anguish and downward spiral.

I had no family or friends in Chicago. I had no one to turn to. I was raw. My loneliness and despair were palpable. Even with medication, I was on the cusp of emotional desperation. I think depression shot out of my eyes and sweated from my pores and was visible for anyone to see. That is, anyone who looked at me, really looked at me. I wanted my brother to be alive. I wanted it to be okay with Harvey again. I wanted my baby inside of me and I wanted Harvey to want to give her to me. I couldn't stay and I couldn't leave.

I don't remember his name. I met him at a local street fair. He was attractive and young and his marriage was also on the rocks. I'm generally a reserved person, but somehow we figured everything out in about fifteen minutes of speaking with each other on the street. He exuded passionate desperation. We must have smelled it on each other. The spark to our attraction was pain. He asked me to meet him for coffee. Innocent enough, right?

I don't think I had ever given Harvey a reason to mistrust me, but somehow that evening he knew. I was on the way to meet my attractive young man. I went to the coffee shop. And for two hours we poured out our stories of anguish, fear and disappointment. He held me and reassured me, and for a brief while I didn't feel alone. We only had one kiss. But it was intimacy.

As I walked back to my car that evening and opened the door, I quickly came to realize that I had made a big mistake and that I would immediately reap the consequences of it. On the driver's side seat was a small crate of car junk that had been in the trunk of the vehicle. Nothing else was amiss. It was a very effective message. It was Harvey. He had followed me. He had been witness and he was letting me know. I wanted to die. By the time I got home, Harvey had already moved out of our bedroom and into a spare room. He left his wedding band on top of the bureau beside our bed.

I sleepwalked through the next several months. I never saw my attractive young man again, nor did I care to. I didn't want him anymore. I had just wanted to be held and reassured and not to be so utterly alone. I was now more alone than ever. As the months passed, Harvey and I coexisted in the same house in a cool and civilized manner. Something vital had been broken. We both felt deeply the bitter sting of betrayal. When Harvey started to go out on weekends in what I'd call club attire, I told myself to be numb and not feel anything. *Just keep breathing. Put one foot in front of the other and try not to think.*

At some point during this "numbing out" period, I reached out to Resolve, a national organization for people with fertility challenges. I became a member and shortly thereafter started a subgroup to support women who were coming to terms with living child-free. Although our stories were all different, they were all the same. We all wanted children and couldn't have them. Although we were strangers, our bonds were instant. Our tie was the seesaw between anguish and resolution. Every month we met and confided deeply personal thoughts and feelings. During the year or so of the meetings with the Resolve ladies, my personal drama played out. Would Harvey and I separate for good? If not, could we rebuild the trust? Could I come to terms with never having my daughter?

Harvey and I floundered for almost two years in this state of uncertainty and civil coexistence. Then, one day he mentioned that he had a job offer in Houston and was moving. He said that he hoped I would come too. It wasn't a collaborative decision. It was a good job, but it was also the means of bringing things to a head. Something had to change, and Harvey was gone within a week of his announcement.

Yes, it was as terrible as it sounds. But, after a while you become so satiated with pain that you don't feel much of anything anymore. You shut down and tell yourself to just keep breathing, no matter what happens next. I told Harvey that I would think about the move while I remained in Chicago and sold our home. Harvey lived alone in an apartment in Houston. And, now I had an apartment in Chicago which I shared with our dog, Gidget. While still living and working in Chicago, I quietly looked for a job in Houston. I lived a secret life which I didn't share with my family, my friends, or even co-workers. I never told anyone that Harvey and I were separated and that we had sold our home. Or that I was considering a move to Texas. With Harvey, I acted like I was willing to make the move to Houston when I found the right job. But, I believe we both knew that I was buying time in order to make the biggest decision of my life.

Little did we know at that time, but our troubles would soon grow much worse. Within a few months of Harvey's move to Houston, he needed surgery on his spine that could no longer be put off. He returned to Chicago for the operation. This wasn't his first spinal surgery, and he was hoping to be back to work in Houston in a month or so. But, something went very wrong. It took the doctors more than a week to figure out that Harvey had a raging staph infection deep in his spine as a result of the operation. But, by then, Harvey was paralyzed from the waist down and began to have seizures. He spent weeks in the hospital and then a rehabilitation hospital on an antibiotic of last resort, you know, the kind that if it doesn't kill you may cure you.

I think Harvey was more afraid that he might not make it than I was. I can't know what it was like for him to have lived the nightmare that he had to endure; but I did know that I had lost faith in his physicians, who seemed mostly concerned about avoiding a lawsuit. And I knew that I had to stay strong so that I could make the best possible decisions for Harvey's care. I wouldn't allow myself to fall apart. There would be time for that later. Although Harvey made great progress in the rehabilitation hospital, it was a long recovery, both physically and emotionally. But, for a while this terrible ordeal did seem to push all other concerns away and during his recovery Harvey and I became closer than we had been in a long while. I could have lost him.

Eventually, Harvey was able to return to work in Houston. I still lived and worked in Chicago, but he returned regularly to visit me. And, I checked out Houston. Although we still loved each other, we again continued to practice at living single. Finally, about ten months into this living arrangement, I got a job offer in Houston, a good one. It was time to make the decision. But, first I had to be sure that I understood the questions. It wasn't as simple as, "Should I stay or should I go?" But rather, "Could I live my life child-free with Harvey, and not regret it, and not resent him for it?" I committed to giving an answer regarding the job offer in two days, on Friday. I was in a panic. The Resolve ladies tried to help, but this was a life decision which only I could make. The night before I was to give my answer regarding the job offer, I still had no answer to the real question. But, I was sure that in the morning, push would come to shove and an answer would become apparent. That didn't happen.

When I made the job call on Friday, all I could do was ask for the weekend to decide. I promised that I would have a definite answer on Monday morning. That weekend was agonizing. I wrestled with my life decision and came to realize that there was only one remaining question: Did I believe that Harvey *wouldn't* or *couldn't* give me a child? If it was *wouldn't*, then it was about our relationship and Harvey's love for me. If it was *couldn't*, it was because—in spite of our bonds and Harvey's love for me—it would have truly ruined him and ultimately have been the wrong thing for all of us, baby included. I damned the strength of convictions.

By Monday morning, I was totally wrung out and worn down. Maybe that's what it took, a real stripping away, to get to the heart of the matter. I was laid bare, but I had my decision. And, for the first time in years, I had a sense of peaceful quiet. That was followed by incredible relief and a burning desire to finally move forward with my life. It was clear to me that Harvey and the boys were my family. In spite of everything, I still loved Harvey with all my being, and more importantly came to know, really know in both my head and my heart, that he also loved me that way. I believe that Harvey would have given me a baby, if he could have. It must have hurt him deeply that he couldn't. We shared a deep anguish over unfulfilled expectations. When I took the job and moved to Houston, I told Harvey that I wouldn't hold the baby issue over his head. To do so would have surely destroyed us. I didn't want to hurt him. I had not only love for Harvey, but at long last, also forgiveness.

It's been fifteen years since I made that decision. My childbearing years are now behind me. And, although it was a long grieving process, it was a necessary one. I had to come to terms with a lot of loss. It hasn't been easy, but it has gotten easier with time. My need for a child has been mitigated by my love for Harvey's sons, special relationships with nieces and nephews, and by volunteering with organizations that cater to the needs of at-risk kids. I now also have a daughter-in-law and a beautiful grandson. I am at peace with my decision and don't look back with regret. My life with Harvey has been even better than I imagined. He is a protective and caring partner. He adores me, and I know it. And, although I will never hold my daughter, I can still love her. There's a small place in my heart where she will live forever. I am truly blessed.

The Stray Thought

Photo by Jane Williams

Arm in Arm—Botanical Gardens, Rio, 2006

Jane Williams

Ipanema Beach

Brenham, Texas 2006

On LeBlon Beach, Rio, 2006

The Williams family

The Stray Thought
Jane Williams

This miracle didn't start out looking anything like the world changer it ultimately became. It began quietly, a stray thought, the kind that wanders into our unguarded, just-waking moments. But persistently, over time, this thing that began as a glimmer reappeared and grew. Sometimes inviting, sometimes frightening, the shape and details of the mental images it painted changed over time. But regardless of its instability, one thing was certain: I could not have imagined six years ago what that single stray thought would, in the end, produce.

I was forty-nine, twice divorced, and childless. Two cats. A comfortable town house in the middle of Houston. Satisfying career, great family, fantastic friends, and a sometimes-interesting love life. While I was by no means well-to-do, I had enough discretionary income for serious travel and reasonable indulgences. No regrets or unrealized dreams.

I am a believing person. To be clear: I don't buy sanctified hankies from TV evangelists, don't breakfast with imaginary apostles—no religious paraphernalia. But I pray, read the Bible, attend church. I talk to God. And, God talks back. Over time, I've learned to recognize God's messages. They start out like champagne bubbles in my gut, then rise to my brain like gentle clouds. But despite their delicate form, God's messages aren't speculative. Silent and unseen, these divine ideas are more real than substance. They have the weight of gravity.

I had never experienced the baby lust that had overtaken so many of my friends in their late thirties or early forties when, after achieving professional success, they realized they'd "forgotten" to have kids. So, no one was more surprised than I when my gut whispered as I was praying one morning that I was going to adopt. *Crazy*, I thought. That wasn't God; that had to be something else—funky hormones. But this idea had the undeniable feel and clarity of a God message.

Still, I dismissed it. The idea, however, would not dismiss me. It persisted, rising to the surface over and over during the weeks that followed, establishing roots. I had to acknowledge it. When I did, it terrified me.

I decided to take the notion out of my head and on the road. The test drive led straight to the great pragmatist of the Williams tribe, my sister, Sandy. She is the soul of careful prudence—which is perfect because I am the soul of careless abandon. Between the two of us, I figured we could make sense of this thing.

And so I ran it by her. She looked silently at me for a moment, the unspoken bubble over her head reading *God, she has gone 'round the menopause bend*—then said "Bu-u-ut, you're just learning to play golf!" Please, do not rush to judgment—my sister is a woman of depth and sensitivity. But golf was and always has been the lingua franca of our family, spanning our political, religious, and financial differences to join the Williams in a single, common cause—hitting little balls with sticks into little holes.

"You don't stop living just because you have kids," I argued. "I can be a mom and maintain my own hobbies and pursuits—I can still be me. People do it all the time. It just takes organization." This time the unspoken bubble over her head read, simply, *Idiot*. What came out of her mouth was, "but you're forty-nine! You have no idea how much work this will be!"

"I'm forty-nine, not decrepit!" I protested. "Besides, I wouldn't adopt a baby. This would be a kid! A girl. You know, a *mini* me!" I started laughing. Sandy didn't.

"You work ridiculous hours." she persisted. "How's that going to happen when you've got a child? Parenting's not some after-hours job. It owns you. You are *never* free. And you have been really free for a long time."

She shouldn't have said this. When she did, a picture popped into my head of me, caroming and pinging around in the heavens like a free radical, high over an efficiently whirring atomic village beneath— a vision Marc Chagall could have painted, calling it *Old Hippie Dream*. Her words had the unintended effect of strengthening my intentions. Maybe I had been too free for too long? Maybe it was time to retether? What better way than to become a nucleus myself, with my own little electron in orbit.

After too much discussion about the expense of raising children and other cautions, we parted. I promised her that I would proceed carefully, no sudden moves, no hasty commitments. She waved me off, wishing me well, telling me she knew I would make the right choice. But, as I turned back to wave once more, I distinctly made out that silent bubble over her head again. This time, it was reading *Delusional moron.*

Despite my sister's less-than-enthusiastic response, and my own ambivalence, the idea would not die. Yes, I was ambivalent. That nagging voice that tries to discourage us from rising to meet challenge—don't you hate that guy? Let's call him "Bummer Guy." Bummer Guy had strong opinions about the idea, feeding me a steady stream of panic: "you're too old, you're too self-indulgent, you don't have the perseverance to see this through." Bummer Guy kept telling me that motherhood was all wrong for me—too permanent, too unalterable. Much as I wanted Bummer Guy to just stick a sock in it, I couldn't dismiss his criticisms entirely. It was true—having a child would obliterate the heretofore guiding mantra of my life—travel light.

But, inexplicably, despite Bummer Guy's best attempts to sabotage my fledgling plans, I continued preparing, continued reading, Googling, gabbing adoption. *I will not let my fear of the unknown or fear of change prevent me from moving forward,* I repeated to myself. Good words. But, even as I psyched myself up, I kept feeling familiar rumblings beneath the surface—my inner commitment weenie searching feverishly for the exit sign.

I ran the idea by so many people that eventually it took on a life of its own. People began routinely asking me about "the plan." I was too embarrassed to tell them the truth: "Yeah, well, about that. I decided I really don't want to cook macaroni every day of my life for the next fifteen years. I don't want to spend my evenings sewing Halloween costumes, working on science fair projects, or drilling for spelling tests. And I really don't want to volunteer myself into poverty again (law school had cured me of any notions that self-imposed poverty for the greater good was ennobling). Just forget I ever said anything." Nope, I couldn't tell them all that. And, I knew that if this was really God's plan, I would not be allowed to quietly abandon ship.

So, on a crisp Saturday in October 2004 I walked myself into an adoption workshop. I already knew I wanted a five-to-seven-year-old girl—not a baby. Aside from the difficulties of keeping up with a toddler in my fifties, I didn't want to burden a young woman in her twenties with an aged parent. But, at the workshop, a sobering truth emerged: a court's decision to terminate the parent-child relationship over the objections of the biological parents usually has a lead time of several years, at least three to four prior instances of extreme, documented abuse, and twice that many Child Protective Services caseworkers and foster homes along the journey. And Texas was not unique. Viewing the biological family unit as sacred was the guiding philosophy of the day throughout the entire American judicial system. That translated into a grim prognosis for me: any child I adopted was bound to come with overflowing baggage of rage and mistrust. I knew, as a single parent, I would not have the stamina or resources for that kind of rehab project.

So international adoption began to look like the only feasible option. What would be different about that? My theory: there were older, adoptable children in Third World and economically emerging countries who were relinquished for adoption because their parents couldn't afford to feed them—no drug addiction or sexual abuse issues. And, there would be more of these kids to choose from. In my mind, poverty was benign; it wouldn't leave any long-term damage that three squares and Nordstrom's couldn't fix. This reasoning may have been naïvely flawed, but it convinced me to think globally.

Too, in the back of my mind, I still half hoped I would be too old, too divorced, or too broke to make it through the adoptive red tape of other countries—and that would be the end of it. I could abandon the course with dignity intact. But, as it turned out, there are countries who allow divorced, solo people over fifty to adopt. No chance of being eliminated that easily.

Still, my fear and ambivalence held me back. For months, I continued on in self-imposed stasis. If anyone asked how plans were progressing, I was full of excuses: "wow, I've been really busy at work" or "oh, gosh, all the Christmas hoopla—gotta get through it and back to it." Sometimes, I just rolled my eyes, implying agencies, red tape, medical issues were to blame for my stalling—you name it, I blamed it.

One morning, I woke up in a particularly foul mood. I was tired of being in limbo. As I showered, I fretted: how could God drag me into something I had so many misgivings about? Maybe I was misunderstanding the meaning of the message? Maybe God meant I was supposed to adopt another pet? OK, that made more sense. Or maybe just foster a child—maybe that was it? Maybe volunteer as a Big Sister? Oh, hell, nothing made any sense. In that steamy shower, I yelled: "Okay, if you want me to adopt a kid, I'll do it—but you are going to have to hit me over the head with it. I need more assurance here about how this is going to work. Where is my heart for this—for that matter, where is the money for this?" I unloaded on the universe and let it know, in no uncertain terms, that the ball was in its court. This decision was officially off my shoulders. I felt better, lighter, as I dressed, ate, read some paper, petted some cat, and sped out the door to work.

Thirty minutes later, I walked in the door of the office, past my assistant, Debra. She was engrossed in her computer screen. Her first word to me was "wow" instead of 'hi."

"What's so interesting?" I asked.

"The company just announced they've doubled their adoption benefit," she responded. Coincidentally, Debra and her husband, Erik, were also considering adoption. However, unlike Debra, I had not shared my plans with anyone at work. My neck and ears prickled with heat. I asked—well, more like sputtered: "adoption benefit— what adoption benefit?" My lips were dry, my heart booming.

"Oh, yeah, it's an employee benefit—five thousand dollars per child toward the cost of adopting—you didn't know that? Right, why would you? Anyhow, they just doubled that to ten thousand dollars per child—can you believe it? Omigosh, wait'll I tell Erik!"

Shutting my office door behind me, I leaned against it. A great, whole-body laugh poured out of me, and I realized I was feeling as dizzy as if I had, in fact, been hit over the head. The next year was spent completing paperwork, psychological testing, domestic studies, etc. While my fear and indecision had not vanished, I had moved forward and around them. The end of the year found me trying to adopt from Brazil.

Why Brazil? Actually, choosing Brazil was the easiest decision. In 1999, there were approximately eight hundred thousand children living in the streets of Brazil. By 2005, the numbers had not changed significantly. These street children were either orphaned or so impoverished that their chances of survival were better on the streets than in the *favellas* (shantytowns). The reality of street children is universal, but, what made the plight of Brazilian children unique was the culture's solution for dealing with them.

Between 1988 and 1990, 4,600 Brazilian street children were murdered. Twenty percent of these children were murdered by police. Children and adolescents burglarized shops for everything from food to electronics for black-market fencing. The country didn't have the infrastructure to address the problem. Merchants, left with no options, resorted to self-help. They hired death squads, manned by off-duty police. These vigilante squads earned up to fifty dollars per street child they killed. When nine-year-old Patricio Hilario da Silva's body was found, a note was tied around his neck. It read: "I killed you because you didn't study and had no future. The government must not allow the streets of the city to be invaded by kids."

Suffice it to say, Brazil had older kids to spare. So, with this knowledge and a dozen guiding "coincidences" pointing the way, Brazil became my natural choice.

Here's how choosing a child worked: After all my paperwork had been submitted, the agency I was working with started sending videos of kids from Brazilian orphanages. The kids were dressed up in their best duds, parading around in front of the camera, giggling and waving, blowing kisses. The girls would prance, flirting. The boys would joke around, making bodybuilder poses. An adult interviewer would be talking to them so you could get a sense of each child's personality. Each one of them was selling it as hard as they could, desperate to become part of a family.

Some of these kids' parents had died. But, most had been living on the street and by the greatest of good fortune, were picked up by the authorities. How you might ask, in a sea of street dwellers, would one child stand out as being worthy of notice and intervention? If that child was being beaten, abused, sold in plain sight—these circumstances could warrant calls to the police from concerned witnesses to these crimes. Or, maybe sometimes, they were just lucky.

It didn't take long to figure out that none of the older kids came solo. They had siblings—anywhere from one to five of them. And, it was Brazilian policy to try to adopt siblings into a single family whenever possible. Was I open to the idea of two children?

It turns out I was. I first applied to adopt two sisters, Isabella and Isabel. They were six and seven, sweet, dimpled, with eyes like dark chocolate truffles. I submitted the petition and waited. The news came two weeks later: the girls had been awarded to a French couple. I was disappointed, but certainly not heartbroken. "Oh well," I told myself, "the Brazilian sea was full of little fish."

I applied for a second pair of sisters, Regina and Hortensia, ages six and nine. Both were animated and charming. Their video showed them coloring at a table with their friends. Joking, laughing, their good natures were apparent. Again, I waited. And again, my application was rejected, as the sisters were awarded to yet another French couple.

Two rejections in two months—it was all the excuse I needed to detour from the process—a reprieve—a chance to live a bit more of the good old life. My reluctance once again assumed the lead. Why, you must be asking, was I doing this at all when my heart was so clearly lukewarm? I asked myself this many times as well. All I can say is that emotions were not the driving force behind this decision.

I continued reviewing videos, but all sense of expectancy was gone. Time passed. I dallied, passively floating in and out on the tide of everyday life, going nowhere.

One night, returning from the grocery store, I saw shadowy movement on the dark pavement ahead of me. As I neared the spot, I made out that it was a cat. He had just been hit by a car. I pulled over, grabbing a shirt out of the back seat of the car as I jumped out. The poor little animal was wild with pain and bewilderment. He was desperately trying to get his bearings, to breathe, to keep living. I knelt beside him, tying the shirt around his abdomen, attempting to staunch the flow of blood. I hoped there was enough fight in him to make it to the animal emergency clinic. When I touched him, he didn't claw or bite. I picked him up gently to carry him to the car. And as I did, for a second, our eyes met. At that moment, on that street, my hands soaked in this little animal's blood, a thought shattered my consciousness with clarity: *Life turns on a dime. There are no guarantees. It's scary. It's miraculous. Each moment of it is holy. You were put on the earth to love. Stop wasting time. Go get your kids.*

I was shaking as I put the little cat in the back seat and sped to the animal emergency clinic. I ran with him into the clinic but already knew it was too late. He was gone. Leaving him at the clinic, I drove home. Coming in the door, I walked to my computer and wrote this note to my adoption counselor: "It is time for me to get my kids. I will do whatever it takes to make this happen now."

Terri, my counselor, called me early the next morning. "Wow, what's happened?"

I answered. "I just know that it's time. Let's get this done. Whatever it takes."

"I believe you; just give me the morning," she said. "I'll call you back." At noon, I called her back.

"OK, do you remember Bruno and Bruna da Silva?" she asked. "We got their pictures three months ago. No video. Just a snapshot and a short report from the orphanage?"

"Sort of. I think so," I responded. I looked through my folders, pulling up their picture and report. Kids from Recife, a large city in northeastern Brazil. Bruna was eleven, Bruno was nine. They had been at the orphanage for about eighteen months. Before that, they had lived on the street with their mother. They had different fathers—both dead.

Looking at their picture again, I was surprised I had been able to forget them. Bruna was a classic beauty, with a cascading tumble of black curls and luminous black eyes. Bruno was tanned, broad shouldered, grinning—all boy. "Terri, are you kidding? No way I'll get these kids. They are too beautiful. I'll bet all of France is petitioning for them."

She laughed. "Yes, they really are special, but not many people want kids this old. And, the mother's rights haven't been terminated. I spoke to their caseworker this morning; she doesn't think they'll be eligible for adoption for about another six months."

"Oh," my heart sank. That was a lengthy wait; things could happen between now and then. And, I had never considered adopting children this old. And a boy? I could hear the familiar strains of my indecision warming up in the orchestra pit of my stomach.

"Look," Terri said, "if you will commit now, I think you stand a real chance of getting these two. You'll just have to wait six months. I know you've never really considered kids this old, or a boy—all I can tell you is that you're the only one that can decide. Will you do it?" Terri asked.

I gulped, I hesitated—but only for a moment. Then, despite their age, despite their gender, despite the potential wait, with 100 per cent certainty, joy and relief, I said: "*Yes*. If it takes six months, then it takes six months. I don't care that they're older. I will love this little boy. Count me in."

My firmness must have thrown her, because Terri herself started to have doubts. "Really? You haven't even seen a video of them. Don't you want me to try to get a video?" My behavior had her off balance.

"Nope. These are my kids." I said. And I meant it.

"OK. I'll let their caseworker know." We ended the conversation.

Eighteen months of skirting heart-deep commitment rapidly disappeared from memory. I began imagining life with a girl and boy. Having grown up with two brothers, I had a good idea of what it would be like with a guy. A lot of chest-beating, coyote-howling, rough knocks, broken stuff—fun. Sure, they were older—but what is faith for, if not for leaping? And, with luck, we might all be back in Houston, as a family, for Christmas.

Before lunch, Terri called.

"You're not going to believe this," she started.

"Please don't tell me a French couple got them," I begged.

She laughed. "No. I don't know how this happened. But, the mother's rights were terminated yesterday. They're ready to be adopted now. Can you send me your signed petition right now? And, can you be in Brazil in two months? Remember, you'll be down there at least a month. Maybe longer."

"You'll have the petition in an hour. Yes, I can be there in two months. Help me find someplace to live."

This time, the petition took. Bruno and Bruna were mine. On July 10, 2006, my plane took off from Manaus, a city in the middle of the Amazon jungle, on the last leg of the journey from Houston to Recife. It was late at night. The plane hummed quietly, its course tracing the great river that ran beneath it. Lights were out in the cabin, and all was calm. As I gazed out on a full moon and starry sky, a stray thought once again invaded my peace. I laughed. It was Bummer Guy. But he was different this time. I guess by now, he knew there was no turning back. The best he could do was admit, with what sounded like grudging respect: "I never knew you had it in you."

Two days later, I met Bruno (later *August Bruno*) and Bruna (later *Julianna Bruna*) in the kitchen of the orphanage. They were tiny, bony, dark, and covered with lice. August had warts and smelled of rotting teeth. But Julianna's enormous black eyes sparkled with excitement in her delicate face. And August grinned and danced—the littlest, he wiggled, demanding to be noticed. They were beautiful. They had made cards for me on which were scrawled in English, *Hello, Mommy* and *We are a family*. Not much was said—"Hello, hello, how are you?" we repeated over and over. We were overwhelmed. We began immediately to learn each other, touching and smelling each other's skin, burying our noses in each other's hair. They laughed. I laughed and cried. Julianna moved under my arm, and August crawled on my lap.

Conventional wisdom says adopting older children is risky. Characters are indelibly imprinted, parent-child bonds are made or unmade by the time a child reaches the age of five, right? Grim prognostications abound on the topic. So, even as I signed on for August and Julianna, the most I dared hope for was that we had a chance for an unconventional, but hopefully loving relationship with each other.

But conventional wisdom is not infallible wisdom. I had expected to meet strangers the day I met August and Jules. But these children were immediately and deeply familiar. They were mine from the beginning, as surely as if I had witnessed their first breath. And it has always been that way, through good times and bad.

What was it like returning home to real world obligations, raising these children as a single parent, these children who spoke no English, who came to me with unimaginably complex, troubling histories? It was frustrating, exhausting, and humbling. Lots of second-guessing, tears, and, often, choking fear.

Tackling the effects of years of neglect and deprivation was daunting. For two years, life was an endless cycle of physical, academic and emotional catching up. Basic appliances were a wonder to these new Americans; the kids had never seen a microwave, dishwasher, hair dryer, or even a clothes dryer before coming to the U.S. Landing from the flight back from Brazil, I promptly lost August in the Miami airport. He was finally discovered, standing mesmerized in front of a Rube Goldburg-style soda dispenser. Foods were different; they became nauseated at the smell of their first Thanksgiving dinner. Underwear, table manners, basic hygiene—all had been superfluous fluff until their new lives, when this fluff became a regularly enforced part of their day. Learning how to maintain material goods was a huge issue for two kids who had never had toys or clothes of their own. And man, were they rough—! About half the furniture in the house became kindling within months.

At first, they clung together, needing each other, appreciating each other's familiarity. But this survival huddle quickly gave way to ruthless sibling rivalry. Minor squabbles escalated into slug-fests in seconds. Julianna was adept at igniting August's temper. August was adept at igniting her pants (with her in them—not a good afternoon). Each one privately lobbied to send the other back to Brazil.

Regressive behaviors were the norm. Bedwetting, sleepwalking, night terrors, thumb-sucking, tantrums, biting, hair-pulling. They were two-year-olds in bigger, more coordinated and powerful bodies. They were scary.

And always, we kept smacking into the language barrier. The kids used The Great Language Divide to their advantage whenever they could. English phrases like "time to brush your teeth" or "Are you wearing underwear?" were unintelligible to them. But "I hate you!" "This smells bad," and "You're not my mother!" They had those phrases down.

But I learned what I guess all parents learn: there are no hard and fast rules. Each kid is unique. Successes come out of instinct and faith. And, humor. If you ever meet my kids, ask them to tell you their first American knock-knock jokes. Ask August to tell you about the time I tied squash peel to his arms and legs with dental floss (old Amazonian wart-removal remedy). Ask Julianna about cleaning the "chicken" (kitchen). And ask her about *The Texas Big-Hair Style Show* that we directed at an orphanage in Recife, with four little disabled Brazilian girls as models.

During those first, acutely painful years, comic relief would appear with stunning timeliness. Invariably, just as at least one of us was contemplating how to dispose of the bodies, something funny would happen. Someone would let out a riptide burp, or come out with a particularly funny Portuguese-to-English interpretation, or a dog would emerge from the kitchen with a pizza-smeared snout. And we'd laugh hard and relax, homicide averted. Those times were like the cavalry, charging into the massacre just in time to save our scalps. We relished those times, reminding each other of them when we desperately needed glimpses of our better selves.

I figured if we could just keep suiting out and showing up without killing each other, it eventually had to get better. And it did. I gave them room to mourn losses I couldn't understand. They gave me time to shift from self-absorption to inclusion. And, little by little, knock-knock jokes started being funny. Food became familiar, then requested. Julianna stopped dressing like Carmen Miranda. August stopped wearing the Michael Jackson glove. They grew and put on weight. The lice retreated. Teeth, eyes, eardrums and lungs were repaired, and the most stubborn warts finally came off with duct tape (yep). We got a bigger house. We got dogs. We went camping and biking, skating and beaching. We told each other our stories. And eventually, each of us began sleeping at night and letting go of things better left behind.

So, what does that stray thought look like today? Well, like piano lessons and dance team. Soccer playoffs. Slumber parties. Impromptu conga lines. Monster Truck rallies. Lots of cookies, popsicles and pancakes, and the basketball team in their sleeping bags on the floor of the den. Late-night Monopoly and poker parties. A fridge-door art gallery. Water balloon wars. Sunday dinner with Aunt Chris and Uncle Cal. Cooking with Tia Mercedes. Holidays with family. Two goofy dogs. Two long-suffering cats. A tender-hearted "super-jock" of a guy, with eyelashes like awnings. A crazy beautiful girl who loves cowboys, photography, dancing and endless texting. A story about second chances. Three people who love each other and what they have become together. Everything.

Seven Scenes from Shared Space

Afternoon on the screen porch

Mary Margaret Hansen

Seven Scenes from Shared Space

Mary Margaret Hansen

I

The sun is falling lower in the sky and summer's heat is weeks away. The screen porch is cool. A mockingbird, doves, and a jay call out across the ravine. A distant Weed Eater and barking dog intrude.

Life is good here on the screen porch. We talk intermittently. He is drawing. I am writing. We've eaten the cheese, emptied a bowl of olives, and drunk the wine. That may be our supper, unless I rally and sauté mushrooms, drop two beef patties into a hot pan, and pull arugula from the refrigerator. That would be a real supper. Followed by bed, where we have the choice of watching an episode of *Wire* from Netflix or falling into each other's arms for the third time since last evening to commune, to find parts of ourselves long lost or never uncovered or newly blooming.

I move to sit on his lap, astride, my arms around his neck. "Long ago, when I was married," I said, "I wanted to write, but there were the children and a husband, the house, school science projects, and the PTA. So there was only time to write titles for stories that surged or meandered through my head as I carpooled and cooked. That was it." My writing comprised a list I called, 'Titles to Stories I Never Wrote" which I read aloud to my husband one night with both trepidation and eagerness. He abhorred every word, thought the titles vile, or perhaps simply believed I'd tipped over the defined edge of decency and wifehood. Or suspected I was having an affair.

But this man of mine, now, laughs hard and deeply and makes a request to read those titles. This man with slow hands who takes my breath away, time and again. All is quiet except for the doves and faraway traffic. The screen porch expands to hold this moment.

II

"*Use* my studio during your summer break? You would like to *use* my studio?" The words hang in the air, waiting for him to answer, to offer a reframing of his request. For the record, I haven't used my studio in six months. It is overrun with remnants from *Second Seating*, that art installation which occupied me for over a year. My studio space is mine, even though it is still so overloaded that I cannot begin new work. Clearing this space for myself, or for another, will be a huge undertaking.

I hear his request and I have countered. With prodding, he changes the verb from "use" to "borrow" and anchors the word with provisions. Borrow for six weeks. Until classes begin after Labor Day.

He looks at my ten-foot-long worktable with drawers of flat files at one end. It is a complete mess. "That'll work," he says.

I am outraged. "I thought you painted on an easel." Which I assumed he'd bring from storage. For six weeks. Until classes begin once again.

The man is honest. He wants the space to do his work. Enough of the dining room table. I had my first studio in the 1980s. This current studio space of mine is but two years old and he is about to take it over. I feel like a lioness, protective of the artist in me.

But it's just for six weeks. Does that make a difference? Maybe. He loves me. Yes. Am I a nice person? Maybe.

I begin to sort and cull, organizing this space so that the man I love and who loves me can paint. For six weeks. Tell me, how exactly do you sort through a Pyrex baking dish that's filled with chandelier crystals, spools of thread, torn photos, a tube of Super Glue, a package of needles, rubber stamp pads, glue sticks, a sliver of glittery fabric, a bottle of metallic powder? How do you categorize things that could all make it into the next piece of work?

It takes me hours to clear and organize this space. That was yesterday. Today, he is already in my studio with the vacuum cleaner. The man is ready to paint. He is restless. He has not painted in four days. This man is mine. Doesn't matter. Space is space.

I, with my bolts of fabric, piles of clippings, pages of typed words, thousands of photos, gelatin molds and Bavarian plates, Chinese paper cuts and Mexican pots, strange buttons and beads, Turkish scarves and metallic sandals and daughters and grandchildren and very old parents and a new year-long art consulting job, will loan my studio space to him.

After all, he left behind his masks and shamans and carpets and most of the accoutrements of his other life. He lives out of small suitcases and striped Mexican bags. He paints and brings the paintings to me like a new cat brings birds to the doorstep. Their feathers and his brush strokes are beautiful.

For six weeks he will paint in my studio and I can watch him do that. I could look on this "borrowing" as a gift.

III

Conversation and his paintings drew me to this man a long time ago. Conversation was intense and always in passing. We were young and married to others and saw each other at dinner parties. After such parties, I'd climb into bed beside my husband and reflect on our fleeting exchanges.

It was then that I bought one of his paintings, secretly. I like the man's work. Always have. Paid for the painting out of household funds. The gallery owner delivered it to my studio, where its energy and mystery expanded and filled that first "room of my own." This man who conversed with me in passing at parties telephoned to say he was curious about the woman who could live with a painting he deemed so dark. Could we meet? I said yes, we could converse and, furthermore, he could see the painting in its new setting.

He arrived in a leather jacket on a cold day and we began a conversation of which I remember not one word. What I remember were his kisses, our kisses, in between the words. We spoke and kissed until I left to pick up kids from school.

The man and his wife left for Rome and then Greece and Crete and Turkey, while I became a single mom with three teenage daughters. They moved to New York. And then he wrote that he was returning to Houston to paint. He would be alone. He was leaving his old life, starting over, he said.

Might he see me? Might we converse once again?

"I am single now," I told myself, "And he will be 'alone' in Houston."

We entered into a heady combination of conversation and sex. I believed him when he spoke of starting a new life, until his wife returned to fetch him and we said goodbye. I cried and wondered what our steamy Houston summer meant.

"Life goes on," I told myself. My daughters grew up and moved away. I bought a house with a garden. I found jobs that were demanding, satisfying, and energy sapping. Good women friends filled my calendar. By design, I no longer listened to rhythm and blues radio, no longer allowed random, fateful stirrings. I let go of thoughts of sex and conversation. Of course, it helped that every year I was older with fewer hormones filling my mind, body, and very soul with lust and longing. I discovered that my days were improbably okay without a man simply because I found my life interesting. I reveled in the lack of compromises one usually makes when there is a man. The years were full. It is quite enough to have work and art and causes, friends and daughters and grandchildren.

And then a year ago, across a spring gala's silent auction tables, I see this man whom I have not laid eyes on in a very long time. He is among the evening's honorees. I still own that painting he deemed dark. How could I have forgotten that it was probable that I would see him at this event?

My first words are not hello. "Are you alone?" I ask.

"Yes." For this evening.

"Then perhaps we can talk?"

I discover that he is still teaching, still painting, still married. He and his wife have a home in Santa Fe, yet he works full time in Houston and commutes.

I have not seen him for so long. I am curious, want to gauge his feelings about our past. "We were good together," I say. "How long ago was that summer?" The years have folded in on one another and I cannot quite remember.

He says swiftly, "Twenty years."

I am stunned that he knows it has been twenty years since we filled each other's arms and covered each other with kisses, that he has counted or kept track of the years that have passed since that summer when night after night we made love and drifted through conversations on art and politics and books and life.

So, he remembers, perhaps even better than I, the heat of that summer. I remembered our love affair without counting years, the number of which would have given it more importance than I could bear. He, after all, left me.

We trade business cards and days later he sends an e-mail, "May we converse?"

I do not answer immediately. Instead, I create a folder and file his e-mail while I contemplate. After several days, I reread his missive, type a one word reply, "Yes," and click Send.

There are more short, cryptic emails and then I respond as I did long ago. I invite this man into my space. He arrives at my house with flowers and a grin. I attempt assembling supper and the food is a mess. I am too undone to prepare anything as he watches me from the kitchen table. I remember nothing of our first evening except that I could not cook and that he kisses the same as before.

He asks if he may see me again.

Of course.

I make an appointment with my gynecologist, she who for years concerned herself with annual Pap smears and little else.

"I am about to become sexually active," I tell her. This sounds so clinical, so I add, as if it mattered, "I knew him long ago. We've reconnected." Still clinical. My gynecologist takes a look inside, prods my belly, speaks of vaginal atrophy, and offers Premarin for dryness. Dryness? Atrophy? I also think she smiled and said I'd be okay.

This man who clearly recalls making love twenty years ago arrives on my doorstep again. He does not bring flowers a second time. I boil shrimp with garlic and red peppers that we peel and eat from a colander. The kitchen table is loaded with lighted candles. Our minds are elsewhere. I cannot invite him into my own bedroom. Not at first. I offer the bed in the guest room.

And to this man whom I have not been with for twenty years, I say, "I am *so* glad that we've made love before. I just couldn't have sex with someone new. Not at this age." I am hoping good memories will carry us through. I feel absolutely virginal and I tell him so. I have no idea what will happen. I look at him and see that we are both older and say, "Thank god, you knew me when I was forty." Heaven knows what he is thinking.

I am in bed with this man who can remember how we fit together, who loves to kiss, who can talk and have sex at the same time, who can fuck with his mind as well as his body. We meet each other's eyes and cannot believe we are together again or what it means and where this will lead.

Sex is good. I am happy and relieved. There are consequences, though. We make very good love over and over and my body is totally unused to this sort of thing. I begin a regimen of Tylenol every six hours so that I can stagger out of bed in the morning, walk across the room, bend over, drive the car, move through my days. Muscles I have not used in years are under siege. I do not tell my Pilates instructor, though I am sure she could have offered strengthening exercises.

It is late spring when he says to me, almost reluctantly, "I think I am falling in love with you." I am happy to hear that. I am getting used to sex, and the Tylenol regimen has ceased. I can also cook again, without burning the vegetables or breakfast sausage. I think I may be falling in love with him, too.

He calls me "darling," a term of endearment strange to me. No man ever, in my life has called me darling.

In bed one afternoon, I tell him that when I left my full-time job, it was not to retire, but to spend the next ten years doing things I'd put off for decades. I told him I had a list and was very busy indeed. "You only go around one time in this life," I say, "I don't want regrets when I'm eighty-five." I speak quietly and firmly, as much for myself as for him.

It is almost a year since the gala where I saw him across the room. It is also quite late at night when he calls to say, "I'm all yours."

"Whatever do you mean? Where are you calling from?"

"She and I are getting a divorce," he says. "I told her that I love you, that I've loved you for a long time. I listened when you said, 'You only go around once.'" I am stunned. I wonder where on earth we are headed.

"Can you pick me up at the airport tomorrow?" All of a sudden I need to pick this man up at the airport and drive him to the space where he parked his own car in a city lot?

I see him standing there without a jacket, carrying a small bag, looking vulnerable. He has taken a leap into the unknown. Somehow I am in the unknown with him. What does "I'm all yours" mean, exactly?

Weeks before his fateful decision, I spoke jumbled words across the breakfast table, "I've been wondering what it would look like if we were together, really together." There was a pause, "We'd have to have two households. I hope you teach forever. I really like my own space. I really like living alone. How would we 'be' together?"

We'd fallen into a schedule of busy workweeks, each of us going our own way, interspersed with languorous weekends. The walls in my house became covered from floor to ceiling with his work. This does not overwhelm me, because I coveted his paintings always. They mingle with my photographs and quilts and stones and books. We learn ever more about one another. There is no guile, no pretense. We've become a couple. Making love in the guest room is a distant memory. We are used to sleeping with one another in my very own bed.

IV

Tonight I am restless. Summer's heat is intense. I've returned from visiting family in Seattle and my days are busy with work. He is sound asleep and I lie sweaty beside him. I cannot hear the air-conditioning compressor, so I know the ceiling fan is the only source of moving air. The skin is raw in my vagina. No sex for two weeks makes a difference in this older body. I search for that tube of Premarin.

Still not sleepy, I reach for a flashlight and use it to read *Vanity Fair*'s take on Elizabeth Taylor and Richard Burton, fabled icons. I read the words that Richard wrote to Elizabeth and they remind me of words now spoken to me. The sleeping man beside me has declared he is besotted, that I am his life. Sometimes that scares me. Where is the space in "besotted"?

My head aches from a glass of red wine. I take two aspirin and drift off until I awake with an ache in my gut. I wonder about food sensitivities, impending heart attack symptoms. Altogether, a restless night, and then I see early daylight. I am sweaty and irritated and worried. He is awake, reaches for my hand and he is hard. I laugh with no mirth. "I couldn't be less inclined." And then I begin lamentations.

I tell him I have not slept well, that my stomach hurt in the night, and that I must call the doctor to schedule an appointment. He feels that I am wet, but the wet is simply leaking Premarin. I throw my arms over my head in defiance. No kissing.

My lamentations do not deter in the least. I succumb. We are chest to chest. I feel his aura like a magnetic current. He is saying words and we are wrapped in one another.

I am in a deep place, deep enough that a long-ago lover flashes before me, bringing great sadness and sudden tears that cover my cheeks. Someday I must go to him and say I am sorry that I didn't recognize love. I ran from it. At this late date, with this man holding me, I am learning not to flee.

Morning sun falls through the blinds. He chants, "Oh, yes. Oh, yes. Oh, my darling Mary Margaret."

I hear my name. Such a Catholic name. I am no saint. He falls quiet and I watch the veins pulse in the hollow of his neck. Tears and thoughts of my long-ago lover fade and I think suddenly of a woman friend. It is as if she were present, her sensuality and appetite for life are with us. I tell this man that an old lover and a woman friend are passing through my thoughts, that they have become part of this morning with him. I can say this and he is not undone. He is trustworthy.

That is why I love the man. He knows me and it's all good. My vagina is open. Again, after two weeks. My headache is receding. Perhaps living with "besotted" will be OK.

The man is sequestered in the living room reading the Sunday *New York Times*, after clearing the breakfast dishes and cleaning the kitchen floor. I notice that my lover cleans the kitchen floor with the same sponge that we use to clean dishes in the sink.

He even said to me, "You don't complain about what I use to clean the floor."

"No," I answered, "I have not said a word, but I did notice that you used the very same sponge that I use to wash off spatulas." I tell him that I simply decided to buy boatloads of sponges and from now on, we will use different colors for different jobs.

I just made the bed, bringing messiness to heel. The sheets and summer comforter were draped over half the bedroom floor, pillows awry. Even his small paintings that hang above the bed are askew and need to be releveled.

He says he has grown fond of the headboard that creaks and signals each tiny movement made in this bed. I can read newspapers and he a novel on Kindle, and the headboard confirms the adjustment of a pillow, a move from back to side.

The headboard is our metronome when making love. We seize the moment and the headboard registers just where we are. I listen.

"You're there," I say.

"Yes." The headboard slams into the wall and the paintings are again askew.

We are going through more sets of sheets these days. I do not like to fold fitted bottom sheets and they always remain a jumble. There were certain joys in living alone. Less laundry for one.

And another joy, well, not a joy, but certainly an advantage to living alone, is the ability to expel gas, to fart without thought, whenever necessary, never holding it in or expending great amounts of energy to maintain its genteel place inside the intestinal track.

One crosses into real intimacy when one can expel gas in a lover's presence. How many times have I walked to the other side of my house and closed the door of the guest bathroom to cover a fart cacophony? Often.

And then one day he farted. In front of me. Not so bad, I thought. And then another day, I totally, inadvertently, unintentionally farted during a burst of conversation. We got through the moment with my hasty, offhand apology.

However, I began to stay put when I needed to expel gas whether in conversation or in bed. I rustled newspapers or became suddenly and loudly delighted with Pink Martini's newest album whenever gas needed expelling.

Then fate declared, "Over with this nonsense. He loves you. You fart. The whole world farts." We are sharing kitchen space, tending to small tasks when he begins, "You are a fine, wonderful woman—" I stand over the sink, perhaps peeling vegetables. Heaven knows where his comment was leading. This fine and wonderful woman bursts into laughter and hears not a syllable more.

No, instead the ripping expulsion of gas blows in gusts as I reel around to face him. I am caught in laughter, confusion and I am, like an infant, unable to control any bodily functions. I laugh, I cry, I fart, and then I pee. On the kitchen floor. There is nothing to be done. He has witnessed a full performance. There is no turning back.

"We are a pair," he says. "You are a delight." Are we nuts?

We have laughed our way through sex this evening. Raucous laughter. I say to him, "How lovely that you appreciate my eccentricities."

"How lovely that you laugh when I am inside you." God knows what's funny about it. What's funny is that we are happy. We laugh because here we are, together, enjoying every moment.

V

"Matisse was radical. He'd never have been able to sell his paintings in Houston." He is reading the Museum of Modern Art catalog I brought him from New York. We sit at the kitchen table as early evening western sun streams through our wine glasses onto dinner plates.

A month ago, he borrowed my studio. We made the borrowing part clear. But now his newest work is captivating me in unexpected ways and I am eager to see where it leads. Days before my trip, he and I unfurled a quilt-like painting during one of those mornings when we unroll canvases that he has stored in plastic for decades. He is showing me a lifetime of paintings, many unseen in any gallery, some forgotten, all now in storage.

A thirty-year-old quilt-like painting flopped open on the floor, dusty and brilliant as gemstones. I fell in love with its strange patchwork and we brought it home to hang in place of the vintage quilt that had graced the living room wall for years.

Now he is ripping up old paintings he'd designated for heavy trash day and is reconfiguring the remnants so that old imagery remains, but more is covered with new pattern and color. They are new, yet terribly familiar.

As for my studio? I tell him I want my worktable back again. As for the easel? It can stay a while. As for the plywood set across sawhorses? It can stay because I love what he is painting in "my space." At this moment in time, I'd rather have his new paintings than "space." And, after all, I am writing. I am consulting. I will reclaim the rest of my studio later.

At last, at the end of summer, it is time to meet (most of) my family. A very big deal in Seattle, where two of my three daughters live with husbands and my four grandchildren, where my sister and her family moved when Houston wasn't "it" anymore, and where our very old and frail parents followed in order to be done with Houston summers and, I suspect, to be near their doctor daughter during their declining years. There's a tribe up there in the Pacific Northwest.

Their meeting this man of mine is *big*. My three grown daughters have witnessed their mom become older, happy, and very busy doing whatever she chooses to do, by herself. They like her that way. They're used to it. Now, she is glowing, and not because she's been scrubbed and covered with honey and cucumbers at the Korean spa, though the look is similar.

My dad is ninety-three and delighted to meet this man. My dad is wont to burst into song, tunes from 1930s and 1940s. On this visit, he is joined by another tenor who can sing and sketch at the same time. Not often can a woman my age introduce a lover to her parents and obtain their approval and, perhaps, outright blessing.

My daughters are happy for me. Yet they also ask, "What about your space?"

They know their mom likes her very own space. Her quiet times. Down times. She's talked about this since their childhoods. Is Mom giving something up for this glowingness? Or getting something more? Or is she able to have it all? And do we care that much?

My friends respond like my daughters. They too are happy for me or say they are envious. And yet from some, I sense cautiousness in their words. Is this what you want? You, who touted the freedom and lack of compromise that come with living all by yourself. I can easily add to what they may be thinking. At last, I built a studio in order to have space for the work that floats through my head. I left a job to do things long put aside. And honestly, I relish flinging both arms across a queen-size bed, sleeping in the very middle. I never felt lonely except when married. A friend wonders if we've all been alone for so long that we might not want or be able to compromise. Sex would be nice, she says wistfully, but what else would we be getting into? My friends and I enjoy living independently. What kind of women are we?

So, I am indeed wondering about "my space" and about sharing my life so intimately. Yet this man is easy, invariably interesting and continuously paints good stuff. We engage in heated, meandering conversations and so much sex. And there is the wonder, always the wonder that we found one another. There is that pull we are calling love.

We come and go, leave and return. It seems to work. As we go to sleep together at the end of a busy week, my butt pushes against the small of his back. We are warm and comfortable.

VI

"The thing is," I say to him as I look across the dinner table, "there is so much I want to do. So much." I look directly into his eyes. "I am sixty-eight years old. I am not thirty-five. And any of the things I pursue could be a whole career."

I began to enumerate. "I want to find warehouse space for another exhibition, and I'd need to raise money to do it."

"These new paintings of yours remind me of collages that live in my head. Mine are about photos and stitching and words and nostalgia. They've been there for years now, waiting."

"I have to earn some money, so I sure hope there will be another consulting job after this one is finished."

"I want to travel with you," I say, "and you are seventy-one. We have a whole new life."

"And then," I say emphatically, "There is the book."

He knows. "There is the book."

It is time to live every single moment of the present, to share, to talk, to see, to make love, to paint, to write. Seize these moments.

VII

Through the blinds, in the darkness so close to dawn, I see the morning moon in the western sky, round and bright. I rise from bed to raise the blinds as he says, "Let's go out to the screen porch. I'll make coffee."

In our robes, we lie on the old metal day bed, propped up on pillows damp with dew, watching the moon slip slowly down through the trees. It is dark and very quiet on the screen porch. There are no birds singing, no air conditioning compressors. Only white noise from the distant freeway. The moon is brilliant as the sky lightens ever so softly.

We are quiet on the porch until I ask this man of mine, "What *is* this?"

"Darling," he says. "Love. It's love."

He's right, and this time around I know it.

My Husband is Retiring

Getting a look at the Methodist Hospital Research Institute's new building

Susan A. Lieberman

Liebermans at home

My Husband is Retiring

Susan A. Lieberman

In thinking about transitions, I am flooded by memories, sweet and bittersweet. Walking our youngest child to kindergarten stands as a major transition but, in my case, not one that had me brushing away tears. I nearly skipped home, joyous at having a few hours of time alone in my house.

When we packed that same child off to college, I knew we'd miss him deeply, but I wasn't sorry to see him go. First, he was desperate to be on his way, and I was excited to have the freedom to immerse myself in work after two decades of disequilibrium that came from never getting the personal/professional juggle into perfect balance.

Significant transitions kept coming. Birthdays ending in zero. Weddings. Grandbabies. Leaving my busy job and realizing I wasn't just pausing; I was, in fact, retiring. An ill mother. These were all moments, shifts from one way of being to another. But they all seemed to me to be part of an expected unfolding—normal chapters in the story called My Life.

But now, I am coming up on a transition that doesn't feel like another chapter but another book. In just a few months, my husband of forty-one years is retiring. My husband, Michael—the Energizer Bunny, the fretter who always has work on his mind, the guy who bounds out of bed before the sun, is out the door by seven, and gone for twelve hours—is planning to stop bounding and hang out in our house. "Didn't you think one day he would retire?" a friend asked. Since he is on the cusp of sixty-nine, I suppose retirement is a reasonable possibility, but no, I didn't expect he would retire.

When I married Michael, he was as much in love with his laboratory as with me. I couldn't imagine either love affair ending. The early years of our marriage were shaped by his unspoken but obvious need and desire to find success as a research scientist. And although I sometimes resented the time good science required, I was complicit in his goals. But in the middle of our marriage, I vividly recall our having a fight, a big fight. We never argued much, so this argument stood out. I don't know what started it, but I remember stewing in my study long after Michael had gone to bed, and then waking him up shouting, "The last eighteen years have been great and I want eighteen more, but I don't want the same eighteen. I want us to grow and change."

He must have heard me on a deep level because we did change. Michael had been the poetry editor of his high school yearbook. He loved poetry then and considered majoring in literature at Yale. However, a professor assured him he had no talent, so off he went in the direction of medicine and biochemistry. After that disruptive evening, he began writing again and had a serious affair with his muse. In writing poetry, he reclaimed his emotional life which he had, in great part, delegated to me when we married.

Over the years, Michael's need for time alone and his ability to focus intently on his own interests sometimes irritated me, but with the wisdom of hindsight, I now realize it benefited me greatly. It encouraged me to develop my own career, my own interests. I became accustomed to being alone, even when we shared the same space. I started making decisions without consultation. In short, I have had the pleasure of a deeply satisfying marriage with a man who has made few demands on me, and who has given me the freedom to do as I choose and enough money to do it. Michael makes me laugh and never bores me, and I know he has my best interests at heart. It was my husband who urged me to quit my demanding but fulfilling university job. "I think this gig is up, Suze. It is making you angry all the time," he observed.

Michael is excited about not working. Healthy and still energetic, he is eager for the chance to live his own life, unencumbered by the big responsibilities he currently has as chairman of pathology and head of the research institute at a major hospital. This included overseeing the construction of a new building for ninety scientists, their equipment and staffs. He sees my freedom and it looks good. He wants time to write poetry, to work on his Spanish, to exercise in leisure, to think and explore and go the museum on a Tuesday afternoon when it is nearly empty. He wants to find out what larger self might be living in him that has not had the opportunity to emerge.

I'm excited for him. He has earned this. He is entitled to the same freedom I have loved. Yet I'm terrified. It seems a bigger transition than sending our boys off to college or even off to wives; bigger than turning sixty or leaving my mainstream career.

Why, why does this feel like such a tectonic shift, I have been asking myself. After all, he will still be an introvert when he retires. I'm sure he will still spend time alone in his study, writing, reading, thinking. I don't think he will expect me to make lunch. So, why does this feel so big?

First, Michael's retirement signals to me entry into our last developmental stage. Perhaps we don't look like what younger adults call old, nor move like old people…but we are in the process of becoming old. Heading into our seventies, we are rounding the bend for the last act, and while I was clear about the general plot for those earlier acts, I have no script outline for this one. I understand that old doesn't mean boring, infirm, slow-witted or even slow-moving. It describes a chronological moment and that moment cannot be bent backward by plastic surgery or yoga. I can change how I look and how I think, but I cannot change where I stand in time.

Second, we have been blessed to see our resources grow with each decade. Now, we will begin to see our resources decline with each decade. There are, I think, enough resources, but it's such a different way of being and it scares me. This isn't about real money but about existential money: about becoming comfortable with living from savings rather than saving from earnings.

Third, as much as I often wished for more time with Michael when he wasn't exhausted, now, I am nervous about his expectations. Simple, reasonable questions like: What are you doing today? When are you going to eat lunch? Do you want to go to the gym? may make me feel cornered. Since leaving the university and returning to writing and consulting, I am often alone in the house. I wander. I might sit at the kitchen table 'til mid morning, sipping tea and reading the *New York Times*. I eat caloric food standing at the kitchen counter without feeling as guilty as I should. In the late afternoon, if I have been out with appointments, I can curl up in the library with a book and slip into a nap.

The idea of sharing my house—well, really our house, but on weekdays in daylight it has always felt like my house—unnerves me.

Forty years of living with a partner who has been distracted by his work have made me comfortable with solitude and independence. I seem, after so many years of marriage, to be commitment averse— that is, averse to committing to a schedule. What if I say I am going to the gym at two p.m., and then I get lazy and sit with my book instead? My private laziness is one thing; displaying it to someone else— even if that someone else isn't judgmental—feels bad. What if I commit to eat lunch at noon and then decide to have a muffin with coffee at a meeting and don't feel like lunch— and Michael has waited. I know I am making my husband sound like some sort of control freak when he's not at all. Michael will read this and wonder why his being in the house should make me feel constricted in doing any of this. This is all about me and my fears—not a me that seems particularly attractive on paper, but me nevertheless.

On the other hand, here is a huge opportunity. It is like being in our twenties, newly married and deciding where we wanted to live and how we wanted to work and what shape our lives would take. We will get to ask those questions all over again. Amazingly, the questions seem more important at the end than at the beginning when I was too naïve to understand their import and how enormous the choices were.

When we first married, I realized that even in marriage we remained separate people. We didn't read each other's minds, dream the same dreams, want the same choices. Now, it all feels less separate. How else could I end up writing a memoir that features my husband? After forty-one years of being together, writing about Michael is writing about me. Both literally and metaphorically, he has penetrated me. His "moving home" is every bit as much about me as about him. I know him so well that sometimes I know when he is horny or hungry or unhappy before he does. His vibrations perturb my own. And I love him so much and care for him so deeply it is difficult to ignore his needs when they conflict with mine. That doesn't mean I am always loving. Sometimes I get angry when Michael hasn't yet asked for anything. I'm angry because I have anticipated "the ask" and the difficulty I'm going to have in deciding how to respond before he's said a word. Understandably, he regards this as a bit nuts, but it is perfectly clear to me.

So now, in just a few months, there will be this huge transition for Michael as well as for me. It hasn't happened yet on the ground, but it is happening in my mind just now and filling my thoughts.

Crossing the Rubicon

Illustration by Donna Siegel

Donna Siegel

Crossing the Rubicon

Donna Siegel

Marriage has no guarantees.
If that's what you're looking for,
go live with a car battery.
　　　　　—Erma Bombeck

Growing into who you are genetically destined to be can cause a lot of problems. Especially if you marry when you are nineteen and you haven't a clue as to who you are or who you will become. For example, I met my husband during the first month of my freshman year at the University of Iowa. He was a junior. It was 1949. We were with other people at his fraternity's fall dance, but we both felt a magnetic attraction. It might have been what people call love at first sight.

He was across the room when I spotted him. I thought he was very attractive: flashing white teeth, erect carriage, and there was that riveting, inscrutable way he looked at me. I wasn't surprised to see him work his way over to where I was standing and begin a conversation. That's all it took. After that, we were together nearly every afternoon and every night, studying in the library, seeing a movie, talking, and watching the ducks in a nearby city park.

Larry (we all called him Sonny then) was elegant and worldly. In addition to these significant qualifications for husbandhood, he wore cashmere sweaters, had impeccable manners, ordered expertly from a menu, and always remembered to pull out my chair at dinner. I wish I could present myself as a deeper person, one with better values, but I don't think you're supposed to lie in your memoir. In my defense, may I point out I was then a shallow eighteen-year-old, who had only recently matriculated from her dancing stage into her full-bloom upward mobility stage.

Actually, that wasn't all I admired about Larry. At nineteen, he was amazingly mature and grounded. Maybe that was because his future was clear: he knew he would live in Davenport, a town only sixty miles from Iowa City, and go into the family jewelry business. I, of course, had no plans at all. I was the first woman in my family to go to college, and, although it seems strange now, with women firmly entrenched in every profession, my generation had very few models of independent women with careers outside the home and even fewer models within our own families. In fact, my Uncle Ray's parting suggestion to me was to take liberal arts classes because they would make me a well-rounded wife, capable of interesting dinner table conversation.

Larry and I glided into our relationship as effortlessly as the nearby ducks floated on their pond. We seemed to be a perfect match. A few months later, in his senior year, Larry was elected president of his fraternity, and I was voted the fraternity's sweetheart. We met each other's parents and were married six months later during Thanksgiving break.

For the next twenty-five years we followed the plan. We moved to Davenport, we produced three healthy children, we were active in the community, had great friends, and the business flourished. We seemed to have everything. But we were missing one thing: a close and intimate relationship. And the problem was magnified by the fact that only one of us seemed to be missing it. Me.

Maybe that's why marriage counseling didn't work for us. Through the years we tried everything. We participated in several rounds of marriage counseling, alone and together. We tried a trial separation— during which time we dated each other. We followed that by joining a Marriage Encounter class—after which half the class got divorced, including the leader. We did better at Masters and Johnson, the renowned clinic in St. Louis, where we were such a big success we were dismissed early. Unfortunately, we had to leave our idyllic surroundings and go back to the real world.

Things came to a head when we built our Pineacre house. I imagined we would live in it the rest of our lives—that was the dream I was building along with the house.

From the beginning, the house was regarded as my project. I found the plan in a magazine and worked with an architect to modify it to fit our needs and the shape of the lot. Larry was remodeling the store at the same time and was too preoccupied to take much interest. A perfect metaphor for our marriage.

The Pineacre house turned out to be a nightmare of *Mr. Blandings Builds His Dream House* proportions. Symbolically enough, the house took nine months to build. I was there every day that the men were working and the children were in school—problem solving, trying to cope with hostile workmen who saw me as the enemy, while I saw them as misogynists sharpening their spears on a safe target.

It grew into outright war, and after months of it I was exhausted. I felt totally alone. Being responsible for the biggest budget I would ever have didn't help. At least Mr. Blandings had Myrna Loy for support and Louise Beavers to cook dinner. To keep going, I gave myself locker-room pep talks that Knute Rockne would envy. That worked for a while, and then nothing worked.

When other people talk about the depression they refer to the global economic disaster; when I speak about the depression I am referring to what happened to me. Although I didn't welcome the idea of lifting the lid on what might turn out to be Pandora's Box, I entered therapy. I had to—it was either that or conduct the rest of my life from bed.

Entering therapy turned out to be one of the best things I ever did, but I knew even then I might be committing myself to some irreversible action. What I didn't understand then was that depression—although painful and frightening—offers a unique opportunity to grow. Growth, however, can require you to leave what is familiar, what you may still love.

When Jane, our last child went off to college, it was clear that the last reason for us to be together had just left. The play was over; it was time to strike the set. It was painful to leave Larry, because part of me still loved him—the *him* I married when I was nineteen, and who still reappeared now and then on vacations. And then, finally, he stopped showing up.

It was tough, but I had to accept the fact that the seductive web of exteriority we had spun together was what a marriage was to him. But I couldn't stuff myself back into the role I had clearly outgrown. As W. C. Fields put it: "If at first you don't succeed, try, try again. Then quit. There's no point in being a damn fool about it."

It was strange. Not only had I lost my husband, I had lost my twenty-five-year-old career path. I needed to find a new one, quick. Only one seemed to beckon: that fork in the road I didn't take—the last place I felt I was a work in progress—academia. Up to now, I had taken classes in anything that interested me; it didn't have to be useful. You could even say that useless information was my specialty. Unless, of course, you, like my Uncle Ray, consider holding your own in dinner party conversations that require a smattering of knowledge in philosophy, literature, and the color-field paintings of Jules Olitsky to be useful.

Relentlessly—which is how I pursue everything—I pivoted 180 degrees and pointed myself in the direction of schools offering income-generating classes that might lead to a job. Trade schools, vocational schools, technical institutes, I perused them all. I eliminated rabbinical schools because after a course in Hinduism I believed my Higher Power was located near my solar plexus, where it functioned as a center of Etheric-Psychic Knowing. A lot of congregations can be picky about stuff like that. Trying to come up with something, I went to the library, where I always go when I'm looking for answers because it's a lot closer than the Delphic oracle. This time I skipped the stacks with Proust, Kant, and Julia Child, and went right for Richard Bolles and his classic *What Color Is Your Parachute?* The cover of the book proclaimed it was "the bible for career changers seeking fulfillment." Not just a book for career changers looking for a job, but a job offering fulfillment. That was for me.

In the first chapter, I was instructed to start with an inventory of my skills. That was a challenge, what *were* my skills? Shlepping kids to swimming lessons? Writing skits for Sisterhood fundraisers? Dinner party conversations? In the end, I chose a professional school that offered a BA degree and training in photography. I wasn't sure I had any talent, but I did have some experience photographing jewelry for the newspaper ads I put together for the store. And I had a 35-millimeter camera with three lenses.

I knew that going to a nuts-and-bolts school like this at my age was going to be a challenge—particularly when I scarcely knew the difference between a nut and a bolt—but as my center of Etheric-Psychic Knowledge already knew, even if I didn't have talent, I had the resolve of a pit bull. I submitted a portfolio to Brooks Institute in Santa Barbara and, to my great relief, I was accepted.

I had a direction and a road. Now, all I needed was a major. The classes listed in the catalog offered a plethora of career possibilities:

journalism, illustration, portraiture, film, and, at the technical end, industrial photography. Which one should I choose? Let's see, which one offered no chance for creative expression in a field in which I had absolutely no interest? Which one had nothing to offer but the best chance for a job, albeit in an industrial setting? With visions of bag ladies dancing in my head, I chose industrial photography. There might be jobs in these other, more touchy-feely fields, but I could see that manufacturers and factories all over the country were *actually advertising* for people.

Never mind that industrial photography was clearly the most difficult curriculum. Or that I was forty-seven with nothing going for me but a cluster of totally unrelated skills. Or that I was about to add more totally unrelated skills to the mix—the ability to take stroboscopic photographs of bullets rupturing an apple and drops of milk refracting and falling into a cup.

I could rationalize my decision by paraphrasing Robert Browning: "A woman's reach should be beyond her grasp or what's a heaven for?" But you already know that my decision was totally driven by fear; I was the victim of the bag lady syndrome. Although I had never really been poor, I was pretty sure I wouldn't like it. And besides, as my divorce attorney had pointed out in my first visit to him, I was "unmarketable" in terms of a second marriage. I clearly needed all the help I could get.

My moving company put my things in storage until I had an address in Santa Barbara. I began my odyssey across the country in a newly purchased blue Comet that I paid for myself by cobbling together my income from various writing projects. After two days of looking, I found an apartment not too far from the school's campus that felt right. Fortunately, it came with a couple who was willing to rent the other half of their duplex to a middle-aged student, with no local recommendations and no discernible income.

My new place was charming: Mexican tile in the entry hall and a sunny kitchen, and, just beyond, a large living room and dining room with practical loopy brown carpet. There was even a fireplace (my first) and glass doors leading to a tropical plant filled patio. Upstairs were two bedrooms with a bath in between. From the front guest bedroom, I could see the mountains, and by angling the pier glass in the master bedroom, I could reflect this view right to my bed. My half of the furniture fit perfectly into its new surroundings and it is all still with me today.

Unfortunately, classes didn't begin for a few weeks. Each day that I spent waiting for my new life to start seemed endless. I was totally alone in a strange place. The phone never rang, and no one came home at the end of the day to ask, "What's for dinner?" My nightly entertainment was driving the Comet to the beach to watch the sunset over the water. A crowd gathered there every night to see the show; it was like going to a drive-in movie. We sat on picnic tables and watched the orange ball drop to the horizon, flatten to a top hat floating on the water, dwindle to an egg yolk, and finally disappear into an orange ripple on the water. We all clapped in appreciation every night.

I would have enjoyed the peace and quiet of that interlude more if I had known what was about to befall me once I started school. Brooks Institute, so charming and friendly in the brochure, might offer a bachelor's degree and some occupational skills that would look good on a résumé, but it wasn't going to offer me a gentle transition into independence. Instead of a nurturing climate, it provided boot camp training. I suspected that Nazi storm troopers had trained the teaching staff. We were welcomed on our first day by the school's commanding officer, who suggested we look at the students to our left and to our right. Chances are, he said, we wouldn't be seeing them at graduation two and a half years from now. In fact, he pointed out, since the attrition rate at Brooks was close to 50 percent, we might not be there ourselves.

It didn't take long to see why so many students dropped out. The slightest infraction of a subtle technicality on a submitted assignment—if one's photograph wasn't perfectly aligned on the matt as measured by ominously pointed calipers, for instance—all the hours spent producing the assignment were wasted. "Redo" was the order of the day here, which meant more midnight hours in the damp, acerbic processing lab. To make it to graduation and the Promised Land was going to require all the perseverance embedded in my genetic coding; I could only hope that a hedonist wastrel we were never told about did not cohabitate in my gene pool.

Despite the fact that I was developing alarming clusters of purple veins that were crisscrossing up and down my legs from these all-night sessions, and that my children were older than most of my fellow sufferers, it never occurred to me to quit. I was determined to acquire the credentials I needed to open those doors to a professional future.

That meant I had to master Industrial Photography. One look at my classmates and I knew I was in trouble. All male, they looked as though they could repair their own cars and maybe build a rocket without instructions. This was going to be like expecting Goldie Hawn to play Hamlet's mother. I finally had gone beyond chutzpah—this was in the realm of self-flagellation.

I am going to fast-forward through the trauma of the next two and a half years—the sleepless nights, the constant redos, the weekly calls from my divorce attorney over one thing or another because the divorce was still not final, and the overall feeling I had become the star of a movie called *Alice in Blunderland*.

Let's just say that I beat the odds and managed to graduate. I even turned a lemon into *limoncello*. I managed to find time to write articles and humor pieces for the school newspaper, and the faculty surprised me by awarding me a special scholarship. I also made a lot of young friends who frequently invited me to "boogie" with them on weekends. The years between us melted away. My fellow students shared their secrets, taught me to smoke marijuana (yes, I did inhale), sang songs to me on their guitars, and helped me master the technicalities of my view camera (the ones with bellows and a hood). Once in a while, when we weren't working on a project, we watched the sunset together and talked about the mysteries of life, which now included our still murky futures.

We had a special connection. We had been through the war together and we were the survivors. On the day I graduated, my brother, Rick traveled down from Oakland—where he teaches political science classes at Mills College—to attend the glorious event. I sat in the audience wearing my coveted cap and gown and waited for my name to be called. While I waited, vignettes of my life passed before my eyes.

When at last my name was called, I climbed the stairs to a thunderous ovation. Safely on stage, I turned around to see everyone in the room standing, including the faculty. I could hear shouts of, "Way to go, girl" coming from the balcony. I blinked back tears. I could never have imagined an ending like this. I felt triumph and joy and a little pain. It had been a long and arduous journey, but I was finally standing on the other side of that fork in the road.

Despite the ordeal I had suffered at Brooks, I did go back to school one more time. This time I managed to survive epidemiology and statistics. I even wrote a thesis, which led to my master's degree in public health. My two degrees now hang on the wall of my office, but I don't consider them the end of anything. I'm not sure I have grown into who I am destined to be yet. I plan to be a work in progress until I see that light at the end of the tunnel. I hope that light leads right to the adult education department. A class called *Merging Your Stroboscopic Photographs and Your Etheric-Psychic Center Through the Magic of Photoshop Layers* would be perfect.

Ode to the
Waiting Place

Women in a Waiting Place, 1939

Sandra Wotiz

Playing piano with Blake and Reed

Age 22 dating Lee, 1968

Vacationing from law firm, 1993

Congratulated by Judge Joe L. Draughn
after passing the Bar, 1991

Ode to the Waiting Place

Sandra Wotiz

> *Don't approach your history as something to be*
> *shaken for its cautionary fruit . . . Tell your*
> *stories, and your story will be revealed . . . Don't be*
> *afraid of appearing angry, small-minded, obtuse,*
> *mean, immoral, amoral, calculating, or anything*
> *else. Take no care for your dignity. Those were hard*
> *things for me to come by, and I offer them to you for*
> *what they may be worth.*
>
> —Tobias Wolff's advice to Mary Karr in her
> memoir, *Lit*

I was the reluctant poster child for my generation: get your teaching degree, become an "M.R.S." through marriage, and ride into the sunset happily ever after. Except I never wanted to be a teacher; I just didn't know how to think outside the box.

From early on, I knew I was in charge of my own life because neither of my parents was capable of providing me any guidance that I respected. My mother, a strong, controlling person never gave me or my brother a single positive stroke growing up. She was not a mean or vindictive person. She did not neglect us. She had a good heart and was always dependable, but she did not give us any emotional support or hugs and kisses. After frank adult conversations with her, I finally came to understand that it was the way she was raised; she just didn't know any better. My mother grew up in a poor, large, Orthodox Jewish family where she and her two sisters were considered second-class citizens. College was never an option so she had no chance to broaden her views or horizons. Not only was my mother a woman of few words, but her parents told her she wasn't pretty or smart like her other two sisters so she better find a husband to support her.

She did. She found my dad: a warm, fun-loving man who played around on her from day one. He acted more like an irresponsible second brother to me than a dad. He owned a rough bar in the seedy part of Pittsburgh. I was ashamed of his business so I told friends he owned a restaurant and worked nights. Once my mother found out about my dad's cheating, he made life at home a living hell. Dinners were especially hard since he liked to sulk. I learned to fill in the void by talking nonstop. When he refused to give my mother household money, I became skillful at sweet-talking him into changing his mind. To this day, I am still uncomfortable with silence and tend to talk too much around quieter people. My only saving grace growing up was the encouragement of my mother's two sisters and their two older daughters; they believed in me.

My mother drilled in me that getting a teaching degree would give me summers off and more time to spend with my family. Although we never had a substantive conversation, it did not dawn on me to ignore her advice. Plus, as a 1963 high school graduate, I had no idea there were any alternatives to the three careers most girls were steered towards: teaching, nursing or secretarial work. For financial reasons, I had no choice but to attend Penn State with many of the same people I knew in high school. My plans of starting fresh at an out-of-state college didn't work out. Only one of my college friends majored in something other than education; she was actually an economics major. I was so unenthusiastic about teaching that I avoided taking education classes until I was forced to do so in my junior year.

The sick feeling in my gut after the first day of my first teaching class summed it up: a waste of my education. My sole attempt at independent thinking was announcing that, if I had to be a teacher, I'd teach music. At least I'd learn something worthwhile. My mother's response didn't surprise me, "Why music? You can play the piano, but you're not that good." That only made me dig in my heels to prove she was wrong. I could sing and had played the piano since I was five so how hard could it be to teach music? I had no clue how unprepared I was until I walked into Music Theory I class and felt like a deer caught in the headlights; most students had specialized in music theory in high school. Again, no lights flashed in my head to switch majors. I made it through the music curriculum in two years and graduated.

With my parents' ugly divorce fresh in my mind, I jumped at the chance to avoid going home by moving to New York with a girlfriend attending New York University's social work grad program. Make no mistake: I was determined my life would be better than my parents. I quickly applied to music grad schools and turned down Columbia for NYU for no other reason than our apartment was within walking distance of Washington Square. I loved the city and dated men who were a lot more interesting than the Penn State guys.

I was not good at handling roommate conflicts, however. Rather than deal with something my girlfriend did that bothered me, I withdrew. Apparently I had picked up my dad's sulking habit, but my girlfriend forced me to discuss these issues. I learned to count to ten (sometimes several times) and blurt out the problem. A year later, one of my other roommates and I flipped a coin to see who would tell the new people in the apartment above us to quiet down. I lost and it changed my life forever. The cute guy who answered the door (looking like the typical college freshman in our building) apologized and I left thinking what a waste—he was too young. (After all, I was a sophisticated graduate student!) A month later, he rang our doorbell and asked me to open his beer can since he'd broken his finger playing handball. How surprised I was to find Lee had finished his MBA and moved to New York for a job with an oil company. Who says it's hard to meet people in New York? A year later we were married and Lee's company moved us to Los Angeles for three years, and then to Houston in 1973.

It took a while to get over my fear that Lee would cheat on me. I constantly told myself that a good marriage doesn't happen without work; it takes commitment and mutual respect to survive. It helped that Lee came from a loving family, which was such a contrast to my own family life. Not only is Lee my best friend, but he has always believed I can do whatever I want. He still makes me laugh after forty-one years.

My claims to fame as a music teacher were having Tommy Smothers's daughter and Crystal Bernard, who later starred in *Happy Days* and *Wings*, in my Los Angeles and Houston choirs, respectively. I quit teaching after three years. I applied to the training program at Foley's Department Store and passed their Special Events office on the way to my interview. The name piqued my interest so I poked my head in to ask if they were hiring. By sheer luck, I met the director and she offered me a job on the spot. Who wouldn't like planning fashion shows, makeovers, and Thanksgiving parades, as well as run-ning Foley's Teen Council? This glamorous job paid little money yet required many evening hours so I quit after I had my first son. I tend to make big decisions at milestones and my gynecologist had previ-ously advised I might already be too old by thirty to have children. I became pregnant the first month. Our first son was born on our seventh anniversary. Any anxiety I felt about motherhood—given my background—was alleviated by the strong example of my mother-in-law and the fact that I was willing to adopt the parental approach that built such strength of character in Lee and his brother.

Although accepted into University of Houston's MBA program, I chickened out because I was afraid to take computer science and statistics prerequisites. Fast forwarding through my thirties, I taught piano, played tennis, and had lunch with friends. All this time I kept waiting for some inner voice to tell me what I wanted to do when I grew up. My friends were content to be at home; I wasn't. The only woman I knew attending law school suggested I read Dr. Seuss's book, *Oh, the Places You'll Go!* I was startled to see myself in "The Waiting Place:"

> *The Waiting Place. . .*
> *. . . for people just waiting.*
> *Waiting for a train to go*
> *or a bus to come, or a plane to go*
> *or the mail to come, or the rain to go*
> *or the phone to ring, or the snow to snow*
> *or waiting around for a Yes or No*
> *or waiting for their hair to grow.*
> *Everyone is just waiting. . .*

That was my epiphany. I had two choices: be proactive or accept that my epitaph would read, "She waited forever and nothing happened." I was thirty-nine with another big milestone quickly approaching. But what did I want to do? My first thought was to be a doctor, but I would never see my family, let alone get into med school at forty. While complaining to my brother, an attorney, about my dilemma, I added, without ever thinking this before, "Maybe I'll become a lawyer like you." He laughed and I aimed a silent "Fuck you!" in his direction. I would prove he was wrong. Naïvely, I pictured a pleasant scenario where I attended morning classes at the University of Houston's law school, studied in the afternoons, and spent my nights with my family. Every single male lawyer I knew tried to discourage me. In hindsight, they had valid reasons: age discrimination, long hours, and stressful and tedious work. Recently, my brother, now more mellow and understanding, apologized for not encouraging me to pursue my dreams.

Of course, I didn't expect to catch my younger son's flu and pass out the first night of the LSAT cram course. Feeling cold and nauseous, I left the class to ask where the bathroom was. That's the last thing I remembered. As if in slow motion, I fell straight backward onto the concrete and awoke seeing a cop rummaging through my purse for drugs. I tried to shout "Stop!" but the word wouldn't come out of my mouth. Only when I started throwing up and seeing double did the cop let Lee take me to a hospital. The ER doctor sent me home after a clean X-ray, but the hospital called the next morning to sheepishly admit the doctor had missed my skull fracture and concussion. A real trooper, I took the LSAT that weekend and the law school rejected me around my fortieth birthday. When I was accepted the following year, the dean confided that my excuse for a lousy LSAT score was the best he'd heard in years.

> *I think I can, I think I can, I think I can—*
> *—The Little Engine That Could by* Watty Piper

Okay, so my illusions about breezing through law school didn't pan out. Unless I got good grades, even with a law degree, I might as well plan on playing the accordion in a law firm lunchroom. Before starting classes, I tackled using a computer for the first time. My eight-year-old son was learning to use computers in school. My hope that he would help me master this strange machine lasted one day. When he started rolling his eyes, it was time for plan B. I became best buds with the Apple IT helpline.

My first law school semester holds many memories—mostly bad ones. I walked around in a stupor with English and law dictionaries shoved in among my legal pads and heavy books. I lost ten pounds the first month. For the first time in my life, eating Sara Lee cheesecake for comfort didn't appeal! I started smoking and had several fender benders (who's counting?) which resulted in my car insurance being cancelled. Desperate for car insurance, I finally found some after agreeing to be in the costly high-risk insurance pool with all the sixteen-year-old boys. Clenching my teeth nonstop, I developed a jaw disorder called TMJ which caused constant pain in the front of my ears. My doctor forced me to get physical exercise to offset my ongoing stress. Jogging became my salvation. On Halloween, my husband and sons went trick or treating while I remained glued to my computer typing an outline for my first final. Finishing at two a.m., I triumphantly turned off the computer before pushing the Save button. All my work went into a black hole—never to return. After much crying, I sucked in my breath and started typing again. Funny how you remember things quicker when you type them a second time.

My mother-in-law passed away in November and we flew to West Virginia for the funeral. Lee and I profoundly felt the loss. Once we returned, I grasped that I had lost a precious week of study right before finals. How could I ever forget ruining my six-year-old son's special birthday dinner by incessantly whimpering as we drove to Tokyo Gardens because I was sure I had flunked my first property course. I didn't.

Other things outside of law school changed. My status with men at parties skyrocketed. No longer a stay-at-home, carpooling mom, I instantly became smarter from walking the hallowed law school grounds and was worthy of intellectual conversation. I knew something had to give for time to read voluminous law books. It wasn't going to be my family. I became a recluse and rarely saw my friends; my tennis buddies thought I had moved away or died. For three-and-a-half years, I studied around the clock and missed taking my sons out for Halloween or to the Galveston Dickens on the Strand Festival, which was held during finals week. Lee took the boys to these events so I could have some uninterrupted study time. During spring breaks, I didn't talk to my family during the six-hour drives to and from Padre Island so I could use the time to study in the backseat (I forced myself not to get carsick). Despite relentless guilt trips, these sacrifices seemed worthwhile when I interviewed for clerkships in 1989 in the top 10 percent of my class.

My first interview suit will be forever etched in my memory. We students had to dress the part: dark suit, white shirt, and tie. Thin ribbon ties for women were acceptable. I could handle buying a suit, but no way was I going to look like I came off the assembly line. I bought a feminine white eyelet, mandarin collar blouse and an antique copper pin made from old clock pieces that I was positive would make me stand out. Armed with a résumé that conveniently omitted the dates I attended college and held jobs, I headed off to Interviewland where my clerkships might be awaiting.

Some highlights of questions I was asked (before politically incorrect statements were a no-no): *Just how old are you? Do you have a family? Who takes care of your children after school? Who do you think I should pick for this clerkship: the young man before you who has an MBA and supports his family, or you with your music background and a husband? Perhaps you should look at government jobs so you will have time to be with your family. Where do you see yourself in ten years? Twenty years?* I did not voice the question forming in my mind in response to this last query: When am I eligible for Social Security?

The hierarchy of desired clerkships was law firms, followed by corporations, with government agencies a distant third. I was one of the few in my class selected to interview for a clerkship at a major oil company. I didn't get a clerkship. Later I learned that their diversity program was a powerful influence in their final decisions. I would have thought my background as an older woman would have qualified me as a minority. Guess not. Now don't get the wrong idea. I did get two summer law firm clerkships, but I should have been offered way more based on my grades and interviewing skills. If only the older male law partners hadn't eyed me suspiciously and asked, overtly and covertly, whether I was willing to work the mandated long hours. Perhaps they had a point.

Unfortunately, the Houston law market opportunities in late 1990 took a dive because of an economic downturn. Many students offered jobs after their summer clerkships had their offers rescinded in the fall. I went into my last law school semester without any permanent job prospects. Again, I made the round of interviews. Several law firm litigators secretly confided in me that they were closet-case musicians and believed their music backgrounds enhanced their listening skills as litigators. Luckily, I found a one-year stint as a law clerk on the Fourteenth Court of Appeals.

One of my biggest regrets was missing my law school graduation. The university held just one law graduation ceremony each May and I graduated the prior December. After taking the bar in March, I didn't feel like the graduation ceremony mattered by the time May rolled around. My mistake. My family suffered by having an absentee mother and wife while I was in law school so they deserved the applause and closure as much as I did.

Studying for the bar was a never-ending nightmare. You wake up every morning, study full-time and go to sleep with a throbbing headache. Every night you drive to the bar cram course. So much information was stuffed into my tiny brain that I no longer remembered how to lock my car doors. I had to keep a flashlight in my car to find the side button that says *Lock*. I smoked cigarettes at home for the first time, thinking I was in the clear by constantly spraying air fresheners. Who was I kidding? One son found my cigarettes hidden in my guitar case under my bed and cut them into little pieces with his elementary school scissors. As a bribe to stop my smoking, he left his piggy bank next to the cigarette pieces. When the big day arrived, the man sitting on my right confessed this was his fourth attempt to pass so he was trying prayer this time. The woman on my left had a bucket between her feet since she was afraid she'd throw up-again. Once I took the bar, I never touched another cigarette.

In August, I started my job with the Fourteenth Court of Appeals working for a kind, appreciative judge. I drafted sixty opinions that year and realized I didn't enjoy sitting alone all day in a minuscule office. If I had died in that office, I might not have been discovered for days. Thank goodness for the classical music station that helped the time go by while I typed and typed and typed. Wednesdays were my favorite because court was in session and I interacted with other people and listened to oral arguments.

For the next six years, I worked at a national law firm as a litigator. At first I thought it would be fun being a litigator like the lawyers on *L.A. Law*. I liked the people and learned right away they were clueless about how old I was. My first lunch outing with the young partners was unforgettable. One partner innocuously asked how long I had been married. Like a pro, I quickly replied, "Oh, it's been a while." That tactic didn't work this time. The tenacious litigator asked again, "Exactly how long?" The entire table awaited my answer. I took a gulp of water and answered softly, "Twenty-two years." There was dead silence as the partners did quick math calculations in their heads.

I sometimes felt clueless about the complex business litigation cases I was assigned. Litigation was extremely stressful and, contrary to the secret disclosures of those closet-case musicians working as litigators, my music background didn't help my litigation skills one bit. At the end of the day, being able to think quickly on your feet was the best skill you could possess. I hated the billable-hour dance. Plaintiff lawyers loved to fax me pleadings at the end of the day or, even better, on the weekends. My family got tired of hearing my excuses why I wouldn't be home for dinner. My sons never believed me when I gave them a specific time I would pick them up or leave the office. I am convinced they picked careers outside of law because they lived with a lawyer. Vacations might be scheduled, but no guarantees you took them.

There was the trip from hell. I planned to leave work at noon to drive my sons to our flight to Cancún where we'd meet Lee. A pleading from one of my current cases was delivered to my office at 11:45 a.m. The response was due before I returned from Cancún. Since the buck stopped with me, I frantically researched and drafted a quickie response. I finished at 1:00 p.m. and left to make a 2:00 p.m. flight. The entire time we raced to the airport I repeated over and over, "Shit, shit, shit!" As we ran down to the gate, I knew we had zero chance of making the flight. It was my lucky day; the flight had been delayed due to bad weather.

My final job was as in-house counsel for a Fortune 500 corporation. Corporate culture is a different animal. At the law firm, you didn't discuss your family much; they were allowed to exist, but not get in the way of your work. During my first corporate meeting, the CEO introduced each new employee and asked us to tell about ourselves. I mentioned my law background and sat down. The other employees raved about their families and hobbies. It was okay to talk about your family—and even take vacations. My boss and coworkers were great, plus the work was diverse and interesting. I eagerly switched over to negotiating contracts instead of managing litigation. Never had a dull moment or a day when the time didn't pass quickly. It's a shame my sons were already in college before I had normal working hours. I was there almost ten years and probably would still be there if the company hadn't been bought by a private equity firm that demanded layoffs. I expected to apply for other jobs after a short break, yet, to my complete surprise, I never got around to it. Perhaps I am finally finished trying to prove something to myself.

Would I trade my experience as a lawyer at forty-five? Never. Despite a twenty-year age gap with most of the law students, several became my lifelong friends. I am not the same person I was before law school; I think and read on an entirely different level now. I am better equipped to handle complex matters that may come up in my life. As queen of the geriatrics, I tell other women the unvarnished truth if they are thinking of starting a legal career late in life. Who knows what turns my law career might have taken if I had started in my twenties, when you are confident you can conquer the world. At forty-five, you know better. There were probably other careers I might have liked better or were better suited to my strengths, but I don't have another full-time career change left in me. It's time to stop and smell the roses. And then move on to whatever comes next. I no longer fear The Waiting Place.

Off The Escalator

Photo by Gordon Joly

Kristie Husmann

Off the Escalator

Kristie Husmann

My parents were from the humblest beginnings, both physically and emotionally. As is typical of truly poor people, there was never any help available from their families who also stooped beneath the burdens of life. And it would never have occurred to my parents to seek any kind of assistance. Both of them worked two and three physically demanding jobs at a time, and still every day was a struggle for the most basic needs. I was seven when my mom looked at me and told me if I was ever going to make anything of myself then it would be solely up to me. I went to college on a collection of academic, leadership, and pageant scholarships and studied my life's only dream—singing. But college music programs are designed for people with many years of musical training, which I did not have. Vocal music was for students who were primarily interested in opera, which I was not. It became apparent very quickly that it would be difficult for me to make a sustained living from vocal performance. Particularly the type of living I was looking for—one that was very far removed from my family's lifestyle.

I looked around at the members of the large, prosperous church I had joined in Houston to see which of their career fields yielded the lifestyle I desired. I rejected oil as too risky, banking as too boring, but real estate in fast-growing Houston looked just right. I began work in 1980 at the age of twenty-five with two sweet Christian men in real estate development who had strong principles and who were willing to give me a little training and a lot of patience. I kept the quote from Booker T. Washington at my desk, "Success is to be measured not so much by the position that one has reached in life as by the obstacles which he has overcome." One of the things I learned from these two wonderful men was that commercial real estate professionals in Houston were a small group and you never wanted to do anything that would close doors to you later on—like sue one of them. After three years I was allowed to lease space in a retail center they had just completed. I was surprised to learn, however, that I would not be allowed to do any of the big leases; in fact, I would not even be included in the meetings to learn how it was done. I was confused by that and a little hurt, but it turned out to be such a small taste of things to come. I wanted more challenge, more respect, and more money than I was going to be able to get from our small company. I was also reassured by older friends that I was going to have to change jobs to climb the ladder of increased responsibilities and income opportunity.

After completing enough leases to be "experienced," I accepted work with another shopping center developer in town at quite a large salary increase. An acquaintance, one of the few women in the business at the time, knew the owner and told me that he was a loyal supporter of his church, a trait that was important to me. She encouraged me to take the job. After leaving such noble men that I so respected, I was surprised to learn, too late, that this man had such an unsavory reputation that he had to pay overmarket rates to hire anyone. He discouraged communication, except through notes on colored paper that corresponded with the subject of the note. He would call meetings of all the departments without warning for the sole purpose of verbally excoriating someone (with a maximum audience) over a perceived error. Even simple problems within the organization could not be resolved because team members would hurriedly and passionately point the finger at another person or department—anything to avoid the crippling humiliation that would be meted out over the smallest issue. Midnight calls from this boss were not unusual— for such significant and critical issues as informing me that there were pieces of gravel in the shopping center parking lot that I managed and leased (a center that was located off of a busy gravel-lined country road). Even so, I successfully solved some complicated problems and completed six leases in a couple of months.

For professionals in retail commercial real estate, attending the annual convention in Las Vegas is de rigueur. After walking miles in our high heels to reach our booth to stand on concrete for eleven hours a day, we entertained guests for cocktails and dinner. I was seated next to my new boss who was telling jokes with language that was beyond blue and extremely offensive to women. I wearily excused myself from the table to go to the ladies' room, only to find the sole bathroom on the floor out of order. I made the trip to a different floor, repaired my lipstick, and then went back to my duties.

When we returned to our rooms late that evening, my supervisor told me, "You need to get on the phone and get a flight back to Houston tonight. You are in big trouble for leaving the table and he doesn't want you in Vegas another minute." I was dismissed as soon as they found a replacement, which was shortly thereafter. There was no notice, no recourse, and no severance pay. Technically, the company could have withheld the commissions I had already earned. I was fortunate that the financial officer was well aware of the problem and made sure I was paid my commissions. He also offered to vouch for my performance. I was shocked and upset but not as humiliated as I would have been if I had not known how outrageous this man's behavior was. The benefactress who introduced me to this man went to work for him a couple of years later. After leaving his employment, she apologized to me profusely. Apparently she did not believe my stories and learned firsthand how miserable he was to work for. She told me that he used the example of my dismissal to terrorize his employees each year before the convention. Years later I interviewed with a well-known retail developer who asked me about that company, "Is it true that it was such a tough company that you could be fired for going to the bathroom?" I told him that what he'd heard was my own true story. He was shocked. He had thought it was a myth.

Given my former employer's reputation, it was not difficult to get new employment. In contrast, my new employer was honest, fair and kind. But he enjoyed warning his employees and business associates that he had a bad temper when provoked. To illustrate, he loved to tell the story of what he did to a tenant who put up an unauthorized portable sign. He connected the sign to the back of his car and dragged it up and down the road in front of the center until nothing was left of it. It is important to note that although he had a temper, he treated me respectfully and I enjoyed working with him. One day, however, I was dismayed to come upon a contractor for a new tenant, Mr. X, building out a space. The problem was that it was not the location Mr. X had leased—it was the space Mr. Y, another new tenant, had leased, but had not yet commenced its construction. The cost of ripping out the construction and the delay of rental payments would be expensive for everyone and it meant the involvement of the owner with his short fuse. I solved the problem by arranging for Mr. Y to move into the space Mr. X should have occupied. Mr. Y was happy to do that; the move brought him closer to the major super-market that anchored the center. There was no additional expense or loss of time for anyone. I had legal documents drawn up and signed by Mr. X and Mr. Y that same day, and submitted them to the owner for signature. Although he was grateful, I wondered if he missed not having a reason to blow up.

In 1984, the lure of office leasing with its larger commissions and more sophisticated tenants led me to join a bank's facilities group which was marketing space in a large old building downtown. It was a fantastic job for a few months until the terrible business and financial meltdown in the Southwest. The commercial property market took a dive because of overbuilding and speculation brought about, in large part, by changes in the regulation of savings and loan institutions. Suddenly, space leasing for twenty dollars per square foot was worth half that. Older buildings like mine could not compete with the newer, prettier locations leasing for the same amount. My immediate supervisor just could not comprehend the crisis and would make me deliver proposal after proposal— sometimes to a room full of angry men—allowing me to reduce my effective rate for sometimes no more than a penny a square foot. When I had a lot of empty space to lease, the department head became involved and laid out an aggres-sive plan that I was to pursue, and I pursued vigorously. The depart-ment head was a man who worked hard to build esprit de corps in his department and was a true mentor to me and several other women. Surprisingly (at least to me) he was won over by an aggressive inde-pendent broker whose lavish business lifestyle gave him an aura of success. He was contracted to handle the big deals. I was not allowed to attend his meetings and he took over every important aspect of the job.

Once, when the broker and the department head and I were walk-ing a large block of important vacant space to discuss issues and strategy, the broker ushered me on an escalator (ladies first!) and then led our boss somewhere else to discuss something truly important as I was riding the escalator down and then back up again. He was a master of humiliation and control. The department head told him several times to take it easy on me but by then all the bank's officers had been easily convinced that this man was the leasing savior and he was firmly ensconced. In less than two years he purchased the facilities group from the bank, and gave all my assignments to two women, both of them tall voluptuous, with big hair and very high heels. In conversation, I learned that they did not know how to calculate a lease's net present value. Looking back, I have to laugh at how they affected a roomful of executives. Normally these guys were poker-faced and reticent in meetings. However when these two leasing agents were introduced at a meeting, the men all jumped up to extend their hands in exaggerated friendliness with what I can only call dopey smiles on their faces.

I was unhappy, but not surprised when these two women were given all of my assignments. In the worst Houston real estate market in any one's memory, I was without income. All leasing jobs were commission only, and commissions weren't paid until deals closed. With inexperienced bankers and insurance companies now owning most of the real estate in town, their agents could not get a deal approved for months—frequently after the tenant had leased space elsewhere. In 1989, I decided that the escalator was only going down. I moved into property management where salaries would stay stagnant for fifteen years, until commercial real estate struggled back in the 1990s.

My recollections from my years of leasing and managing tenants feature a large assortment of unpleasant males: an eighty-year-old reeking of moth balls who pushed me up against the wall in an attempt to kiss me, sixty-year-old men who clearly told me I owed them sexual favors for working with them, which they expected to collect up front, screaming forty-year-old husbands going through divorces, thirty-five-year-olds in powerful positions who were as chauvinistic as any of their elders, intentionally excluding women from consideration when filling positions of importance. One memorable character was the wealthy grandson of a powerful family. His board was about to take away his throne (the control of two office towers in a distant city) after his incompetence had driven away large, irreplaceable tenants. He screamed at me for thirty minutes, outrageously accusing me of lying and malfeasance, and then walked out. I found out that he had already, before our meeting, signed the deal I'd brought him. He was trying to assert a last bit of power and control, but succeeded only at being pathetic.

What did I do? I dressed for success, read every self-help book on the shelves, and got two different professional designations, Certified Property Manager for office buildings (with time and work equivalent to a master's thesis) and Certified Shopping Center Manager. I smiled and apologized for getting in the way of that kiss or tried to laugh away the inappropriate advances, approached my job soberly, and always made it the most important thing in my life. Sometimes I went out after work and got drunk and sometimes I just went home and sobbed. I leaned on my friends and sometimes prayed desperately. I looked into other careers, but starting a new career from the bottom required taking pay cuts I could not afford. I had made the decision to try and make a real living and, true to my mother's words, it was solely up to me. Through the years I saw one administrative assistant who frivolously filed a lawsuit against a hapless boss who misspoke at a happy hour. But the company had a powerful HR department that strongly reprimanded him. She did not suffer any reprisals.

Today, thirty years after I began, I still work in commercial real estate, along with vast numbers of women. We are now protected by federal laws, human resource groups, and a decidedly different social consciousness. I still hear some men making the same degrading pronouncements about young, attractive leasing agents in our office that I've heard before. But now, they tend to confine their comments to their male circles, rather than face a call from the national head of HR. I answer to a man I respect, and I do quiet work in a cubicle. I don't deal with office politics, large amounts of money, or people in important positions. I love to be paid to do needed and necessary work and to be left alone to do it well.

Most of the developers I had worked for lost nearly everything in the downturn of the eighties. In the late eighties, I was called by one of the partners from my first job. He wanted to tell me they were sorry they were not able to keep me. Ultimately, they left real estate for other ventures. The bad-tempered developer turned his business over to his son, who was able to change the company and overcome his father's reputation, although he lost some of the assets. The leasing savior spent all of his money and I hear that he is very humble these days, asking his friends for work. The young men who would not interview women for positions of importance were promoted. But now they allow women to be hired, as they are bringing their daughters to work as interns.

The best thing that happened to me during those years was that I met my husband, who, as controller, worked closely with leasing and property management at one of the companies where I worked. He is now encouraging me to pursue a new career. I think of noble jobs, creative jobs, fun jobs. Although change is scary to contemplate, writing this memoir puts the fear in context. I have overcome obstacles, I have attained goals, and I can surely make the next transition.

Growing Up
Outside

Leslie Lee Burris, age 4

Leslie McManis

Growing Up Outside

Leslie McManis

My mother was a forties beauty queen. My father met her when her striking black hair, blue eyes, and remarkable presence won the runner-up title in a Virginia pageant. As the years passed, her body and face became diminished by her own intensity and by the birth and care of nine children. However, our early years together brought frequent reinforcement of her loveliness, and my not quite measuring up. I became, even at a young age, weary and disheartened by frequent comments such as, "Your mother is so beautiful." It was especially annoying when someone would thoughtlessly add, "Now you, you look just like your father." As I grew out of childhood I began to claim some of Mother's beauty by being very proud of her. However, in the early years as I was defining myself, I fell short by comparison.

I was the firstborn. My earliest home life found me overly responsible, lonely, and protective of my siblings. I was also protective and conflicted when it came to my parents, especially my mother, as I viewed her as the weaker one in her ongoing conflicts with our father.

A second child was born with a disfiguring cleft palate. Mother fed milk to the deformed infant boy with an eye-dropper, as he was unable to nurse from a bottle. She refused to visit him in the hospital when he underwent multiple surgeries. When our father brought him home, she neglected her young son in his crib or playpen. Instinctively, I assumed the responsibility of looking after him. His name was Marvin and I was four years old when he was born.

Within eleven months, a third child arrived, a boy named Richard who was whole and beautiful and more fitting for a woman of beauty. Forever after, Mother devoted her attention to him to the exclusion of Marvin.

Mom, did you neglect Marvin because you were ashamed of him as not being a fitting son for a beauty queen? Did my filling the role of big sister relieve you of motherly duties? Since you were raised as the oldest of seven brothers and sisters, did you see my sense of responsibility as natural?

When I was about five or six years of age, my father moved the family to the middle of Pennsylvania Dutch farmland. It was there that children four, five, and six were born. He traveled during the week, leaving us alone and isolated, as my mother had never learned to drive. My mother was too afraid to learn to drive and throughout her life relied on our father to take her everywhere, especially to the grocery store.

Throughout my childhood our father was gone five days of the week, returning late Friday. On Sunday, he would place his packed suitcase at the front door in seemingly eager anticipation of abandoning us each Monday morning. His reentry into the family often gave him hero status because it temporarily freed and distracted us from Mother's despair and her rejection of us.

On my very first day of school, Mother combed my hair and then told me that she would never help me again. From then on, combing my hair, dressing myself, and washing my own clothes would be my responsibilities. I think I got the dressing part down pretty good, the hair combing not so much. The clothes washing was a challenge, as I was not quite able to reach down into the big sink in the spider-infested basement. The neglect was furthered when my parents failed to take me to the doctor for the required first-grade vaccinations. I was suspended for two weeks until I received those shots, an embarrassment for a six year old.

For the first and second grade I walked to a school that was less than a mile away from our house. During cold weather, my teacher, Miss Gearhart, would help me take off my snowsuit with its cumbersome leggings and sleeves with mittens. This began my adoration of my teachers and ongoing role as teacher's pet.

Very early one morning, my unusually agitated mother came into my bedroom, abruptly waking me with the words, "Leslie Lee, your school building just blew down!" A tornado had leveled the school on a Saturday morning. My mother's intense feelings and agitation remained. I, however, calmly rode with my father to view the wreckage, and asked if I could go find my pencils. It was only in adulthood that I realized the full implications of what would have happened had the devastating storm occurred on a school day instead of a Saturday.

Throughout my childhood, I recall numerous times that my mother would shepherd us into the basement whenever there was a thunderstorm. We would huddle in the pump room until the storm passed. Sometimes I would take a contrary position and stay in my room, as if my calmness could quiet the situation.

Not long after the storm, I began attending a school much farther away that required me to ride the bus. Many mornings I would miss that bus, either because my mother had not awakened me in time, or insisted that I eat my soft-boiled egg and toast before I left. On those days I had a long, frightening walk to school. Large farm dogs would come after me or bark threateningly from barnyards. I was such an obedient child that, having been told not to get into a car with someone, I would not even accept a ride from a kindly neighbor, but trudge forward while clenching my fists and holding my breath.

When not in school, Marvin and I were put outside in the backyard while Richard and the other three children were sheltered inside the house. I was always paired with Marvin. Perhaps it was because I had assumed some responsibility for his welfare and always stayed close to him, showing solidarity when Mother's rage and contempt were directed at him. The two of us stayed outside all day, along with my loyal rat terrier. Mother would hand us bologna sandwiches from the back door and we were forced to pee behind a large stand of pussy willows causing the ground to become covered with heavy green moss. Over time, I built a playhouse in the garden near the green pepper plants. It consisted of a large circle of stones that were stacked about five inches high. I squatted down inside of this circle home and prepared green pepper "dinners." Some loving caretakers outside my immediate family had sent me a beautiful flaxen haired doll that came in a silver steamer trunk. In her pink tutu costume, she became my only dinner guest.

Mom, did you keep us outside because you could only handle the other four children? Why was it always me and Marvin? Did you isolate us due to your own sense of isolation? Were you anxious, tired, and irritable because you had given birth to six children so quickly?

When our father came home on the weekends, I could sense that he and Mother had a passionate physical connection. However, the passion that resulted in nine children was also responsible for their frequent fights. Marvin and Richard were often the pawns for their

109

arguments. Sometimes, our father unfairly disciplined Richard while Mother reciprocated by punishing Marvin although neither boy had done anything to deserve it. There were times I was asked to do the impossible. Once, while my father was clutching Mother's arm she told me to go get the neighbors or she would get a gun and shoot him. My father warned me not to move or he would break her neck. I went outside and held my breath.

Mom, what was going on with you two? Did Dad want you pregnant and isolated in order to keep you away from other men?

However, there was relief for me, if not for Marvin, when I was taken by loving grandparents who were affectionate and attentive, and treated me as an only child. I would spend long stretches of time with maternal grandparents Hendrickson at their remote farm in southwestern Virginia. I gathered eggs from the henhouse, always wary of the rooster, and even milked a cow or two under the watchful eye of an uncle. I watched chickens being slaughtered after which they would run about headless before being placed in hot water so that the feathers could be removed. Today I can recall the smell of those wet feathers. I also remember the smell of the slop used to feed the pigs and the glorious scent of rotten apples in the orchard where I would walk with my granddaddy.

My paternal grandparents Burris lived in a town, also in southwestern Virginia, where my grandfather was a Methodist minister and my grandmother a hardworking, sock-darning, practical nurse who made the world's best yeast rolls. I was adored by all of my father's family, while my mother, with her cigarette smoking, and haughty ways was adored only by the men.

But it was even further outside of my immediate family where I received the most consistent love and attention. This came from Estelle and Jack, a couple the same ages as my grandparents, who had been unable to have a child of their own. As neighbors during the early years of my parents' marriage, they would lift me over the fence and keep me for a night or a weekend. Thus began many years of being treated to their innumerable gifts.

Estelle's dinner table was always set with china, silver, and linen napkins each with its own unique napkin ring. In the center, she placed fresh roses from her lush garden, and at my place setting my own crystal wine glass. Through the meals that were prepared, I developed an exotic palate for a child—Danish potato salad, pungent blue cheese, steaks cooked rare and soft-shell crabs—all selected and prepared by Jack. Many a time I bellied up to the butcher counter with him as he haggled for the best.

Tuesdays were Jack's day off and he would bring Estelle a cluster of peach colored gladiolus. After the flowers were presented and arranged, Jack would take my hand and the two of us would head for the zoo in Baltimore to watch the seals being fed. Another scent of childhood is that of the water in the seal compound and the warm sense of belonging that it evoked.

Estelle was a devout Catholic, a fact that caused considerable consternation from the Methodists in my family. She would cover my head with a clean handkerchief and send me to Mass without my breakfast. My nascent young mind ignored the doctrine of purgatory and sin, and focused on the beauty and pageantry of the resplendent churches and cathedrals. I drank in the rhythm of the Latin mass, the porcelain face of Our Lady, the smell of incense, and the sight of flickering candles. The Catholic services, as well as all of the tenderness and beauty that Estelle and Jack showed me, served as a balm to my home life. They may well have saved my life.

Mom, why did you release me to other caretakers? Were you gifting me to them? Were you vicariously sharing my joy? Were you allowing me to have something that you knew you couldn't give me?

Tossing my vitamin pills down the heating grate or hiding unwanted sandwiches behind a large piece of furniture were my only signs of rebellion during grade school years. The evidence was usually discovered when Mother would start heavy cleaning. Imagine the sound of hundreds of vitamin pills going up into an Electrolux vacuum cleaner hose after the heating grate was removed! I felt no pain when my stunned mother began hitting me with that very same hose, and I carefully suppressed a laugh.

During the sixth grade, the family set up residence in my mother's hometown of Pembroke, Virginia. The town was so small that it had no local police—a fact that would become significant given my upcoming short list of delinquencies. Pembroke meant unabashed freedom. I recall little of my brothers and my sister and my mother. I recall nothing of my father at this time. My self-imposed feelings of responsibility for my family disappeared into a joyous independence.

My playmates were mischievous boys. There were early evening bike rides. With me on the back of a boyfriend's brakeless bike, we crashed into a ditch of poison ivy. My teacher, Miss Britt, would take me out of the classroom and into the girls' restroom to help me off with a scratchy dress so that she could apply Calamine lotion to my blisters. My mother didn't provide salve for physical or emotional sores.

On Halloween I went trick or treating with a group of boys. That night we did destructive things such as breaking eggs on cars and windows. And, finding a certain teacher's house, we moved a large planter off the porch and into the road forcing cars to either stop or crash into the obstruction. I had never gone trick or treating before Pembroke and would never go again.

Mom, were you being supported and protected by your family, releasing me from my previously self-imposed duties?

And then there was the fighting with boys.

Lester, a pudgy kid with glasses, made the mistake of pushing and taunting me on the playground during recess one day. I threw a ruler with such deadly force and accuracy into the middle of his back that it knocked him to the ground. The fall shattered the lens on one side of his glasses, sending him crying to report me.

John Henry was an odd young boy who threw rocks at me on the walk home from school one day. I put my books down, picked up a handful of gravel and, with the same deadly force that felled Lester, hurled them at John Henry. After he ran off, I returned to my friends, retrieved my books, and continued home. Later that night the police came to our home. I opened the door to see a patrol car with flashing lights, the county sheriff, and Miss Britt, who said, "Leslie Lee, the children say you were the last to see John Henry and that you were throwing rocks at him. He didn't come home from school this after-noon." Later I was told that he had broken into a church basement and was hiding from me.

I was never arrested or disciplined in Pembroke. It was just a far too brief interlude in my coming-of-age. The family moved again before the spring semester. I entered a new school in the city of Lynchburg, Virginia, and returned once again to a temperate, overly responsible life.

As I progressed into junior and senior high school and then college, surprisingly my mother became my advocate. She made possible many freedoms, in opposition to my father, when she signed blanket permission slips that allowed me to enjoy teenage activities with my friends. My father had become overly strict when I reached puberty, not allowing me to date until my senior year of high school, and then, dictating an unreasonable curfew. My first boyfriend, Charlie, had a marvelous sense of humor and would place an alarm clock on the dashboard of his car when we would go to the local fast food drive-in. When the Cinderella hour approached, the alarm would go off. Our friends in the neighboring cars would cheer as Charlie pulled away from the curb to head for my home, where Dad would be waiting on the front porch.

Mother was also demonstrably proud of me. She praised my poems and short stories that were published in the school literary magazine, and she hung one of my oil paintings in the family dining room. Since she still did not drive, she caught the Lynchburg city bus and came alone to my National Honor Society induction and to my high school graduation ceremonies. She expressed pride in my grades and in my accomplishments.

I don't want anyone to think that I was scarred by my family's early neglect. I see my childhood experience as the basis for a singular self-reliance and gravitas that helped me become an acknowledged leader in the business arena. The shadows—vulnerability and an eagerness to please—are obvious in the photograph of little Leslie Lee four or five years of age, dressed in a snowsuit and posing with one foot forward. She is holding a bride doll. The face is innocent and smiling, as though asking to be cared for. No doubt I've carried this sense of myself into my long and varied working life, sometimes reaching outside of myself for approval when it wasn't necessary. If I were adept at Photoshop, I would scan that photograph of little Leslie Lee with the snowsuit and sweet face and then make her a warrior. A fierce warrior with striking face paint, headdress and fearless demeanor. A reincarnation of her Pembroke self. And a reminder of what she became.

A Closet: Memories, Meaning, and Sometimes Magic

Closet, c. 2011

Mel Gallagher

A Closet: Memories, Meaning, and Sometimes Magic

Mel Gallagher

My eighteenth-century French metal chandelier had no assigned spot in our new townhouse and, since our sons don't share my love of antiques, I decided to hang it in my closet. Countering the electrician's laughter, I referred to it as my "folly," but it's proven to be a wise decision. I enjoy it throughout the day. The soft lighting shows off my clothes, compulsively hung by color and function. It also highlights my collection of dolls (not from childhood, but purchased during the past thirty years); a grouping of family photos (I'm one of five children and thirty-two first cousins); a chest of drawers for mementoes and jewelry (I assign a lot of meaning to certain objects); and a sacred space of old and new religious icons (I remain a practicing Catholic). It's a closet that's brought back memories and given me insights into my life and the meaning and sometimes magic that I've attributed to clothing.

One of these memories was when I was five years old and sat entranced watching my Aunt Jeanne dress for a date. She and her sister shared a bedroom suite with twin closets. They were magical places to me, well organized and filled with beautiful dresses, shoes, and hats. What a startling contrast to the closets in my own home where things were so chaotic that our front hall closet actually had a spontaneous combustion fire requiring firemen, trucks, and hoses. That hall closet is a good analogy for my childhood home: always the fear that emotions would ignite.

Wedding Promises and War Realities: The Forties

Wedding of Interest Today in the Capital Area; Rosemary Ward Bride Marries Dr. Thomas Murphy of Newark, N.J., in Ceremony at Shrine of Sacred

Heart. The bride wore a gown of old ivory duchess satin with a yoke of real Alencon lace. So read the headline and part of a quarter page article on my parents' wedding in Washington, D.C. It occurred, however, on the eve of World War II. From a lavish wedding and promises of an upper-middle-class life married to a general practitioner in Short Hills, New Jersey, my mother's life was abruptly transformed when she found herself married to a Navy physician, juggling eleven moves while having four of her five children during the early forties.

After the war, my father decided to specialize in psychiatry and bought a three-story red brick house, a few blocks from the C&O Canal and the Potomac River in Washington, D.C. Although it was a great home for raising a family, the house was a façade of stability. Even in early childhood, I sensed a disharmony and emotional distance between my parents, a problem that was exacerbated over the years by physical and emotional illnesses, as well as alcohol abuse. "They were wonderful people but married to the wrong person," I would tell a friend later in my life. My mother was a kind woman, loved by all my friends, but her health was fragile. I was awakened by sirens on more than one occasion, horrified to see an ambulance leaving with her. "Your mother's not feeling well" was all we were told the next morning. I was a quiet child, intuitive to a fault, who listened and watched, kept family secrets, sought out a world independent of my family, and learned self-discipline. How I envied classmates over the years who were closely supervised, had curfews, and lived in what appeared to be orderly, stable homes.

School Uniforms and Special Occasions:
The Fifties and Sixties

For my early schooling, I spent twelve years on twenty-two acres in the heart of Washington, where the Sisters of Providence ran an all-girls elementary school, high school, and junior college. I recall donning a brown jumper and brown leather tie shoes for elementary school. Uniforms were not only easy to slip on by oneself, they allowed us to look alike no matter what was going on in our homes. Whereas the uniform was drab, holidays provided a chance to wear something pretty, which in most cases was given to me by my grandmother or aunts. Special occasions came to represent a break from the tension in my family.

I remember the Christmas when I was eight years old. We'd been sent to bed early so that we could be awakened for Midnight Mass. I had been given a new skirt, sweater, and black velvet flats with tiny roses on them. I can close my eyes and be back there, listening to "Oh, Holy Night" at the service. I recently was tempted, but refrained, from spending a fortune on an overpriced pair of black velvet flats with roses, solely because they brought back a positive childhood memory.

Even more magical was my Aunt Jeanne's wedding two years later when I was ten. It was my first trip to a beauty parlor. I remember sitting at the raised head table in the mirrored ballroom of the Plaza Hotel in New York City. I wore a long, pale pink organza sleeveless dress and a floral headband that seemed like a tiara and made me feel like a princess. The experience was like being a doll, dressed to perfection by people who cared.

The only doll I remember from childhood was given to me by Jeanne and another aunt. It was a large Madame Alexander doll in a beautiful red ball gown that came in a blue box. Unfortunately, it disappeared in the chaos of our home. When I bought a Madame Alexander Scarlett O'Hara doll, in a red ball gown, at age forty-one, a psychiatrist inquired if I had always wanted to be a doll. At the time I was peeved, but he was on target. A part of me has, at times, longed to capture the magical feeling I've attributed to dolls, unscathed by the craziness of my childhood.

I was named after my maternal grandmother who exposed me to travel and shopping during the fifties. I often stayed overnight and would go with her on the bus to downtown. We would roam through the department stores and I could sense the pleasure she experienced in finding exactly what she was looking for. It was contagious. I can remember venturing out, my meager savings in hand, on a daylong shopping trip with a girlfriend when I was eleven years old. We shopped for play clothes, and the memory is of the enjoyment of searching for what I could afford. Over the years my grandmother and my aunts also taught me to appreciate the aesthetic of well-made clothes. They would take me along to appointments with seamstresses and I learned how dressing could be creative and fun. I also learned to sew, was given a sewing machine, and made outfits during high school and college.

In high school our uniform consisted of a pale blue wool suit and saddle shoes, and branded us as Immaculate High School students. I do, however, vividly recall two pairs of high heels which represented a rite of passage. One was the black pair that I bought at a shoe store on Connecticut Avenue during freshman year, and the other was a tan pair that I bought in senior year during a visit to New York City with a friend who was auditioning at Juilliard. Despite trouble walking in them after living in saddle shoes, loafers, or sneakers, high heels conveyed a sense of maturity, something I would be called upon to display at too early an age.

I had wonderful friends in high school, threw myself into school activities, clubs, student council. But my home life was imploding and the underlying fear I always felt became more pronounced. When the sirens came at night at age fifteen, my father told me to ride in the ambulance with my mother who was being admitted to the Washington Hospital Center. The sheer terror of accompanying the gurney into the psychiatric ward was bad enough. Watching my mother's embarrassment when an attendant asked in front of me, "Is she violent?" still haunts me today. My mother smiled at me while telling the nurse, "Of course not," and I felt enormous love, compassion, and admiration for her. On the ride home, my father instructed me not to tell anyone what was wrong because "They won't understand." I never told a soul and it became, along with the alcoholism, another family secret.

Hiding—or at least believing I was hiding my mother's illness made high school special occasions, such as proms, problematic. She wasn't able to help me find an outfit, but my older sister came to my rescue for the junior prom. She borrowed a short, full-skirted, yellow organdy dress with shoestring straps from her college roommate. It was beautiful and I felt on top of the world. For my senior prom, I found a lovely woman who, after leaving Cuba, was reduced to supporting her family by working as a seamstress out of her apartment. I purchased a pattern, white satin and white lace material and hired her to make me a sleeveless short dress with a full skirt, topped with a lace bolero jacket that fastened in the back. It may be the most fashionable outfit I have ever owned.

College and Marriage: The Sixties

College counseling was nonexistent at my high school, except for the mandate that one mustn't go to a non-Catholic university. I had dreamt of going to Duke or UCLA. My parents never asked my preference nor gave me advice, so I chose Le Moyne College in upstate New York, one of the few Jesuit schools that admitted women in the early sixties. My aunts handed down to me wooden skis and boots, a blue wool suit, an alligator bag, and an imitation leopard jacket. The skills of shopping that I'd learned from my grandmother came in handy. I took money I had saved from working and went to a small, chic dress shop near Wisconsin Avenue in Georgetown. Being short and skinny (double digit weight), I found great items on the sale rack. I remember the purchases vividly, almost fifty years later, and would wear them today: a gold knit sheath with a matching jacket; a denim dress with a jacket; a burlap skirt with madras pockets; and a grey tweed sheath with buttons down the entire front.

Toward the end of my senior year in college, I became engaged to the nephew of the Jesuit philosopher who had taught me metaphysics and compassionately counseled me through one of my mother's breakdowns. Years later, I wondered whether I'd married the nephew because his uncle had already married God. For the wedding, I wore a short, lace, A-line dress, with three-quarter-length sleeves, and a feathered head piece. It was a sunny day in Washington—Thanksgiving 1966—and I was young, naïve, and full of hope. I had bought the dress off the rack by myself as well as a lovely black cocktail dress for the engagement party my grandmother gave us. Even for an occasion as special as a wedding, my mother was not involved in my purchases, nor in any of the wedding plans. Today, I wonder if perhaps my father just took over, neither encouraging nor giving her the chance to be involved.

When I married, my mother gave me her hand-carved hope chest, imported from China in the thirties. She had let me use it while I was growing up to store mementos. The chest belied the fact that I was far too young to be getting married, but marriage is what good Catholics did at that time if they were "serious" with a boy. My fiancé was studying for a PhD in philosophy at Georgetown. I took a job in a parochial elementary school (as opposed to the better position I was offered to handle adoptions for Catholic Charities), so that our schedules would mesh. We lived in a two-story apartment building in Glover Park, an area above Georgetown populated by young people. None of us had money but it didn't seem important. I remember going to a wonderful dinner party hosted by a woman in law school where the meal consisted of Kraft macaroni and cheese, Pillsbury biscuits, and iceberg lettuce. A girlfriend commented to me during that period that, despite living on next to nothing, I always seemed to have one nice outfit to bring out of the closet for special occasions. At that time it was a white satin blouse and yellow taffeta skirt topped off with a great hot-pink bow belt.

The Bubble Bursts: The Early Seventies

The bubble of naïve bliss was bound to burst and did when my husband failed his masters' comprehensives. He immediately decided, without my input, that we needed to move back to Buffalo, his home-town. The only plus was that there were many college friends living in Buffalo at the time including, strangely enough, the man who would become my second husband and father of my children. My grand-mother was born near Buffalo and she realized what a tough move it would be for me. Her answer was to shop. She bought me a beautiful chocolate-brown coat with a fur collar at Lord and Taylor. Although I loved the coat, it was more her unspoken compassion that I remem-ber. She knew I appreciated beautiful clothes. In fact she'd taught me.

We had been living in Buffalo for two years when my husband made another unilateral decision—to end our marriage. I knew it wasn't working but no one in my extended family had ever divorced so it fell to him to suggest we separate. He had gotten caught up in the counterculture of the late sixties, experimented with drugs, and wanted to move to Afghanistan with another woman. I packed my car and drove two days through a blizzard to Washington. When I arrived home, my father took my mother, younger sister, and me to dinner at a restaurant—The 1789—in Georgetown. I went to sleep only to be awakened a few hours later by my younger sister who had come home from a date engaged to be married—strange timing. While I was listening to her tell me about it, I heard a huge crash. An elderly couple, rather tipsy, had driven into my car. I asked the policeman how much it would cost to repair. "It's totaled," he replied and that is exactly how I viewed my life.

Although I had been teaching and going to graduate school to become a reading specialist, I decided to go a different route when my marriage ended. Growing up in Washington in the forties and fifties, we could not vote in national elections and had no representation in Congress. Although the father of one of my high school classmates was in Congress, we were apolitical. I decided that it would be interesting to work on Capitol Hill, and got a position working for a liberal congressman. My first job was hand addressing two thousand Christmas cards but eventually I worked my way into a legislative position. A photo during the first of my six years in that office shows me in a very conservative dress with a matching jacket. But this was the era of Watergate on Capitol Hill, and I would go through a transformation because of the Vietnam War. Despite having close friends who served in the Marine Corps, I grew to oppose the war and morphed into a more hippie dress style that was appropriate for peace demonstrations and the McGovern campaign.

Second Chances: The Mid-to-Late Seventies

On New Year's Day 1974, I was in Denver visiting friends when I remembered that I had promised to contact a college classmate, Michael Gallagher, to pass along greetings from a mutual friend whom I had seen in NYC. I could barely talk because we had celebrated New Year's Eve with one too many toasts. When I finally reached him, the first words out of my mouth were, "I can't talk." I apologized, but fulfilled my obligation by passing along our mutual friend's greeting, and quickly gave him my work number as a way to end the conversation. I never gave him another thought until he called me one year later.

After law school, Michael had worked for VISTA rather than going to Vietnam and stayed on for a few additional years in the Virgin Islands, where he had been assigned as a public defender. After living a bohemian lifestyle on the islands, he had moved to Denver to practice law. He then decided that he needed the additional credential of a masters in taxation from NYU and planned to stop for a few days in Washington during his move to New York City.

My roommate and I offered him our couch for the weekend and we agreed to meet at a favorite restaurant—Clyde's—in Georgetown when he arrived in town. I walked in and spotted him immediately, sitting at the bar in a blue oxford cloth shirt, jeans, and boots. He was as cute as I remembered with a personality that was witty and charming. I had arranged several dates for him, but we spent the days together and as much time as we could in between our respective dates. We were both smitten and the weekend marked the beginning of a long-distance romance. He was ready to settle down, professionally and personally. So was I and we married one year later.

For our wedding at the Naval Chapel in Washington, I wore a handmade white suit, blue silk shirt, and white hat that I had ordered from a seamstress in Georgetown. My father handled the arrangements for the small family reception, and I have a wonderful picture of him saying goodbye to me when it was over. I sobbed as we left on our honeymoon, which was a two-thousand-mile drive from Washington D.C. to Galveston, Texas, in my yellow Karmann Ghia, without air conditioning. We stopped that first night at the Williamsburg Inn and I still have the soft long white nightgown I had gotten monogrammed for the trip. We didn't have jobs or a permanent place to live but had decided to live in Texas in order to be close to his family which had moved there in the early sixties. We looked for jobs in Houston, Dallas, and Austin and landed positions in Houston.

One of my first interviews in Houston was with a liberal Hispanic democrat on the City Council. I thought it would be a great fit with my years of experience working for a liberal democrat in Congress. I walked into the councilman's neighborhood storefront office smiling, wearing a navy blue silk shirtwaist dress, blue and green spectator heels, and a small bag. He took one look at me, put his feet up on the desk, and never looked me in the eye during the entire interview. I never heard back from his office, which didn't surprise me in light of the enmity I had felt. Instead, I wound up with a government relations position at M. D. Anderson Hospital, where my professional experience, education, and wardrobe worked well.

Widowhood and Work: The Early Eighties

Michael and I had two children. For some reason I can't even pinpoint today, I went back to graduate school at the University of Houston for a masters of public administration when the first son was three months old. I thought this would be an interesting way to spend my "spare" time while raising a family. It took me six years and I sat for my comprehensives while five months pregnant with our second son. It was fortuitous because the degree was an invaluable credential when Michael died of colon cancer. The children were one and six years old. "Everything is okay financially," a friend of Michael told me the month after he died. A year later, however, he called me into his office to disclose that he had lied in order to give me a year to focus on the children and to grieve. It was a kind, good decision on his part.

I had decided to pursue a business degree, but his message was, "You can't go back to graduate school at Rice. You have to get a job -- and don't wait until after Christmas." The truth that he had withheld for a year was that I would have to sell our house if I didn't get a job quickly. I sent out dozens of résumés and landed an interview with a multinational energy company in Baytown. Fortunately, a supervisor at their headquarters opened my letter and résumé since the woman it was addressed to had been transferred. A position had unexpectedly opened when a young staffer, a father of two, was killed in an automobile accident. After two days of one-on-one meetings with various staff, the human resources manager leaned back in his chair and put me on the spot: "Why do you think you are qualified for this job when you haven't worked for the past seven years?" The hostile interview with the city councilman years before flashed into my mind. This time I took the offensive. I talked about my accomplishments: work experience, raising my children, receiving a master's degree, an award for volunteer service, and caring for a dying spouse. I didn't expect his response: "My wife just completed surgery for colon cancer." The job was mine, and he became a strong supporter.

The transition to being a widow with two small children, no relatives in Houston, plus working full time for a multinational corporation was difficult. I hired a woman to work for me full time but grieved leaving my children in her care. On top of that my self-confidence was low, in part because I had always been discouraged from thinking I could do the same work as a man. My father had counseled me to drop out of premed in college, despite being on the dean's list, since as he put it, "Women do not make good doctors and you should never compete with your husband." My grandfather had once confided that my Aunt Jeanne was the most capable of his children, and the only one who could run his business, but, of course, that wasn't possible because she was a woman.

Donning a Corporate Uniform: The Mid-Eighties

A close friend went through her closet and appeared unannounced on my doorstep with outfits that would be appropriate for the workplace. During that first year in Baytown, I recall being at a school board meeting, seated next to the refinery manager, a shy and brilliant executive I came to know and admire many years later. We were both making presentations on behalf of the corporation. I was quite nervous and was praying that I wouldn't be asked any questions; I wasn't. As I was waiting to go to the podium, I realized we were both wearing blue pinstripe suits and pale blue oxford cloth shirts. I wanted to laugh, but our his/her outfits made me feel confident and part of this worldwide corporation.

Over the next two decades, I worked hard and was fortunate to have great mentors, all male, who helped me make the transitions up the corporate ladder. As I assumed more responsibilities, the meetings I attended involved higher-level senior management. Ninety-nine percent were men, and it was important how I dressed. There was a corporate uniform, and I acquired a closet full of the requisite clothing. I seldom wore pantsuits; instead skirts, a few conservative dresses, stockings, and closed-toe high heels. After retiring, I was startled to discover that most of the business casual clothes I wore were at least a size too large. It had been important to blend in and I never wanted to accentuate being a woman in the male-dominated world of oil and gas. Also, for the first decade of my career, I was a single woman in a corporate environment where people my age were expected to be married. My two concessions to femininity were wearing a wide range of large earrings and spritzing myself with Paris by Yves St. Laurent every morning.

Although shopping remained an activity I loved, there was seldom enough time to do it while I worked for the corporation. When I was transferred to the company's worldwide headquarters in Connecticut, I recall taking the boys into New York City for a Broadway show and deciding on the spur of the moment to make a quick pass, if there is such a thing, through Bergdorf Goodman. On the way down the escalator, I saw a rust-colored wool dress on a mannequin. I grabbed the boys off of the moving steps, dashed into a dressing room, and bought it on the spot. It was totally different from any corporate outfit I owned, but I wore it to work anyway. A Frenchman in our department talked to me for the first and only time, "You look chic," he murmured. I was tickled and smiled broadly.

Remarriage and Retirement: The Mid-Nineties to Today

For my third wedding in 1994, to a wonderful widower I met at the corporation, I bought a Donna Karan bright red, long silk dress. Ron had worked in Baytown for his entire career, and I had met him during my first week of orientation at the refinery. I knew his wife and was friends of both for ten years before she died. He had one son and viewed my two boys as an asset. The week before the wedding ceremony, I decided that the red dress was too flashy and opted for a pale blue suit I'd purchased in New York City for business. The conservative approach seemed to quiet some of the anxiety I was experiencing about walking down the aisle for the third time.

During the transition to retirement, eight months after 9/11, I found myself wearing sweat clothes every day. It became my uniform and reflected the lack of any structure in my life and the horror we all felt after the towers fell and the Pentagon was attacked. Without meetings, deadlines, and projects, I lost my identity—and there wasn't a dress code. This coincided with a need to let my hair go gray when they discovered a suspicious spot. It seemed ludicrous to go to a cancer hospital to have something removed and then proceed to put chemicals on it. Suddenly, I was feeling old.

Today, I often wear sweats, but only to work out. I haven't found a style for this period of my life and might not have one. During my corporate years, it was easy to adopt the logic of a man's wardrobe.

Many of the best dressers I knew were men, my father, grandfathers, and corporate executives. Perhaps as importantly, men seemed to control the power. When in doubt today, I sometimes revert to this look. My son recently married and I decided not to follow the advice of a friend to "wear beige and keep my mouth shut." I considered a tight navy blue sheath (low cut), and a fuchsia-colored sheath (low in the back). Sadly, I ended up with a boring pale-blue corporate suit which I plan to sell on eBay as soon as I learn how.

Moving into a new town house and hanging the chandelier in my closet has given me a chance to recall memories, good and bad. Over the years, the clothing I wore allowed me to transition into groups, roles, and responsibilities. At times I believed it could cover up the imperfections I perceived in myself and my life. I recognize that occasionally I have even longed to be a doll, impenetrable to sadness and pain. However, I had also been taught at a young age that shopping and dressing could be fun and creative, which it has been for me. And, like my children who thought, as toddlers, that donning a superman outfit would give them magical powers, I have sometimes felt that clothing could do the same for me. And sometimes, it did.

The Missing Memoir

Editor's Note

The Missing Memoir

Editor's Note

I suggested that she substitute a false name for her true byline. That would greatly limit the number of people who could recognize the unfaithful man in her memoir—his name and occupation were already carefully obscured. After we hung up, I decided to suggest Diana as a pseudonym because of the triangle in the story and a marriage that was, like the unhappy Princess Diana's, "a bit crowded."

Unlike the princess, our Diana is an action-oriented, highly-educated, no-nonsense leader; the role model we admire at work. But she ignored her husband's unloving behavior and her friends' warnings. Her vivid memoir showed her reaching for the tools of her career: research, self-analysis, and outside expertise. The formidable energy, intelligence and resources she mustered trying to save her marriage might have saved a business, but pitting her brain against her gut served only her continuing denial. Finally she realized what her gut had been trying to tell her—she had to abandon her rosy dreams of a happily ever after. Her conclusion would resonate with many readers:

Heads are overrated. I am probably not alone in my ability to talk myself out of things. Nah, Diana, that didn't really happen. Your eyes are lying to you, Diana. But the gut is a funny thing, it does not lie. The body holds mysterious answers. Over the years, I have learned to listen to what it is telling me. The challenges that lay ahead of me: divorce, mean bosses, and all the other slings and arrows I would encounter, could be navigated only by facing the truth. That truth for me can always be found in one place—my gut. When the gut says, "run for your life," run.

Diana is certainly not alone in her ability to talk herself out of being influenced by her gut. The old stereotypes about women being ruled by emotion rather than logic have not been totally dispelled from the workplace. Many of us have advanced in our careers by playing the Un-Woman. We train the left brain to rule. We strategize, rationalize, formalize, and compartmentalize. Like her, we may have become too skilled at overlooking signals from south of our brains. Reading Diana's story is like installing flashing yellow lights in the prefrontal cortex—with a road sign that says: *Hazard! Ignoring visceral warnings can lead to wrong partners, wrong jobs, wrong agreements and other disasters!*

But in the morning, there was an e-mail from Diana. After a lot of soul searching, she decided she would withdraw her memoir. "Too raw," she said. It turns out that her ex-husband is facing a tough and painful battle in the months ahead. The missing memoir was trumped by compassion.

SBW

Why Have I Survived You?

Sue Jacobson

Teenager ready for a dance company performance

Courtney in second grade

With Courtney in 1997, the year before she died

Why Have I Survived You?

Sue Jacobson

Why do I not remember days, only moments?
How do I start.....with the end of my life?

For weeks beforehand I had panic attacks. Was it my new job started a month earlier, was it the fear of failure, was it the overachiever aspect of my personality, was it the perfectionist within, was it my wanting to be the star of my new company? I am a great actress—cool under pressure, love to be the leader, the coach. Stay calm when everything is falling apart around me. A great actress. Then came the horror, desperation, emptiness, and pain.

It was a dark, rainy, gloomy Monday morning. I didn't sleep much the night before after coming home late from a party. I started my day early with panic in my gut, but needed to go to my office on time. So it was coffee, out the door, rushing because I had to attend a very important meeting with you in the theater district at noon. It was nice that the two of us, who were inseparable, were chosen to cochair a fundraising event. Mother and daughter working together. We were excited that it was at the theater. You were a long-time dancer. I was a speaker and took dancing. We loved the stage. It was our time to continue to be a team.

Got to my office and started calling you, no answer. Called your office. "She is not in yet." Called your cell, no answer. Called your office again and they said you were late and it was unusual. Calls, calls, panic, panic. I called your father to go by your apartment. Normally he would argue that I was over-concerned but this time he drove right over. You weren't home. Called your brother to see if he would find you. Nothing. Kept calling your office. Not there. And then I knew the worst had happened. Total terror gripped me. I paced around my desk, down the hall—called—paced—called—hands turned cold—couldn't think.

My employer called me into her office. Your colleagues (my friends) and the police were there. They didn't have to tell me. I knew it, but didn't know details of what happened. Cold, raining, foggy, rushing to office, someone chasing you! Your car spun out of control and you died at the intersection of San Felipe and River Oaks Boulevard, in the heart of Houston's most prestigious neighborhood. Who was chasing you? Why was there no follow-through by the police when there were so many witnesses? We hired a detective, offered rewards, and suddenly the police stopped cooperating. They shut down the investigation. Was it someone from an influential family? No answers, but my gut told me the answers. It was a neighborhood where well-connected people lived. We were a bit high profile, and your company was high profile. It took a long time before I could drive by that corner. It was surprising that anonymous people put flowers on that corner for many months. What lives had you touched?

Remember, I am the actress—calm and cool under pressure, the talker—so I started giving instructions. I called your brother and asked him to go to your daddy's office and tell him. "Dad we have to go right now!" "What is wrong?" "Courtney was killed." They drove home in separate cars, both in shock. I called my rabbi. I called and called and called. Finally my coworkers took me in hand and drove me home. I walked in the back door. People were in the kitchen. I walked into your daddy's arms, tears started flowing, no talking, just hugging, just sobbing and tears.

A group of friends were waiting for me, already informed by both the press and your coworkers. They took my address book and called family. Everyone was there for us. Relatives flew in—hundreds of wonderful people to comfort us. Yet, there was no comfort. Did you know how many people loved you, could you see us? A friend appeared at my side saying, "You do not have to talk or see anyone." After that, I quit talking, panic turned to immobilization and I was numb. My perfect life was over; our family's life filled with joy, fun, and true laughter was over. The days of the perfect family, tears, funny events, the parties at home, cooking together, taking dance classes together, all over forever. Why did I survive you, Courtney? It isn't natural, it isn't bearable.

But what about those panic attacks, or intuition or instinct, the sixth sense, impending crisis? I am a woman who is supposed to have magical powers to incite, motivate. Who am I? What am I now? The road to the future looks empty. For twelve years I have run—traveled anywhere to get away—all over the world—looking for an answer to my questions. Went where you intended to go—France where you wanted to get married, China, walking the Great Wall and learning what you loved of their history, Africa where you wanted to be with the animals, Bali with its simple concepts, or reflecting on top of Cambodian Buddhist temples from the tenth and twelfth centuries. Maybe they would have the answers. You were with me on my quest for comprehension. I didn't care if the areas were dangerous or that the small planes could crash; I had no fear of dying as I had already died emotionally. I still go and go and my heart is still broken. I have been living the life you wanted and trying to be the person you were—meeting people and experiencing cultures from all over the world. Understanding the depth that people do not show on the surface.

Remembering the humor and your connection with students from China, India, and Russia. Remembering the day when you were a little girl and said your new best friend was Svetlana. When I asked you where she was from, you answered "I think Mexico." You had humor in your innocence and creativity. The connections with the international community, the gay community, the performing arts community, political community in D.C., deaf community. Yes, you even learned sign language to be able to communicate with our next door neighbor. As someone said, we are the sum of all the people we have met. You were both the sum and the soul.

When I was forced to go clean out your apartment months later, family came with me. I found the answers you had for yourself. On the side of your bed table was a book called *Random Acts of Kindness.* A page with two sayings was marked: "The beginning and end of Torah is performing acts of loving kindness," from the Talmud, and the other was "The question is not whether we will die, but how we will live."

Friends have told me, Courtney was an "old soul" in thoughts and actions. You gave from your heart, volunteered at Texas Children's Hospital and read to children with cancer, danced at retirement homes to make them smile. But it was the many acts of kindness that I didn't know about until people told me, wrote me, and still tell me, that continue to permeate my heart. The funny, imaginative person you were. Your cousin said you were "a gift to us and the community" and he will always remember your beautiful smile. You were also the glue that held us together. It's the special things you did for others that make me want to fulfill the dreams you left behind—to me.

But how do I drag myself to the weddings and see the babies of your friends? How do I stop crying in the car, to music, to emptiness, to memories? How do I stay away from the cemetery and how do I get myself to the cemetery? I had a perfect life—two children, wonderful husband, great job, fulfilling social life, fabulous friends and then fell into the endless black hole. I never got to say goodbye. How will I survive?

It is twelve years later and we finally moved out of our home, your home and the lifetime of memories. I had to move out or keep running away to all ends of the earth to cope. I couldn't stay there any longer because it was desolate without you. Your father didn't want to leave because he would be leaving you—How would you find us again? Friends of yours and ours still tell me new stories that make me laugh and warm my heart. And then I cry for a life lost, future gone, and my loneliness. I have tried to transition back to the life I had before—seeing more people, working hard, taking on projects—but inside it still feels like the day we lost you. But I am a good actress, so most people can't see my pain. I keep hoping that going through the motions of my old life will eventually get me back to where I need to be, but there is no closure for the survivors.

I became the new mother of your colorful parrot, Zoe, who still chirps loudly and sits on my shoulder. You often commented that this bird was your child and you would never marry or have children even though you sought that life. Was it intuition? Did you sense that you had fulfilled your life and knew you would not get old? You were always doing so many good deeds and meeting so many great, famous, infamous people? You were the happiest when you were tap dancing in those cute costumes. Maybe we are all tap dancing through our lives until we fall off the stage.

Is it true that when you have fulfilled your life, you can die?

Why do I not remember days, only moments?

Lost

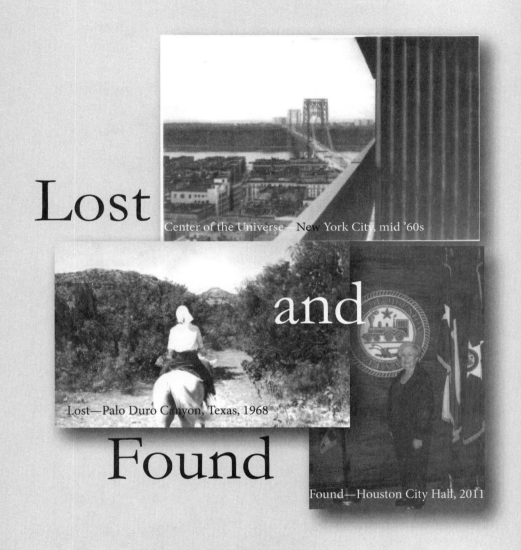

Center of the Universe—New York City, mid '60s

and

Lost—Palo Duro Canyon, Texas, 1968

Found

Found—Houston City Hall, 2011

Madeleine G. Appel

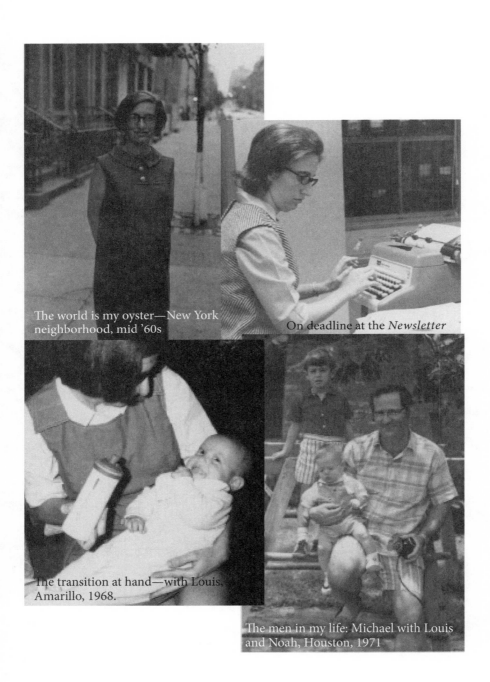

The world is my oyster—New York neighborhood, mid '60s

On deadline at the *Newsletter*

The transition at hand—with Louis, Amarillo, 1968.

The men in my life: Michael with Louis and Noah, Houston, 1971

Lost and Found

Madeleine G. Appel

The most difficult transition in my life to date was my transformation, at the age of thirty, from young married woman without children and with a profession outside the home to young married woman with children whose profession was managing the home.

I grew up in a family where my dad was, on the surface, the wage earner, but my mother held things together. She had an equal voice in all decisions. There was no doubt my dad respected her intelligence and relied on her. She and my dad moved from what they considered the center of civilization—New York and Boston—to the outback of Corpus Christi, Texas, in 1941 just as World War II broke out. My father's brother-in-law, who preceded him to Texas, had persuaded my father that his future lay in managing a ladies ready-to-wear store in what was then something more than a town and less than a city.

My parents had to hire horses and a plow to dig up the clay that became our backyard. They endured infestations of crickets that covered the produce at the local grocery stores. They pined for theater, concerts, and art museums. They grappled with back-country politics and endured endless hot, humid summers. They missed their families thousands of miles away.

But they made Corpus Christi their own. My mother helped found the League of Women Voters and successfully campaigned to end the poll tax and install voting machines. She ran political campaigns. She even wrote limericks to enter in a frozen food contest and submitted anecdotes to *Reader's Digest*. To this day I remember her hope when she mailed off entries and her disappointment when the rejection slips came. I experienced the same hope and the same disappointment years later.

My dad helped found the symphony, ran telethons for the Community Chest, and together they worked with others to create the art museum. I sat in the backseat when we picked up George London, the singer, at the airport; I watched my mother scramble eggs after one concert and put them in front of Claudio Arrau, the pianist; and I fretted with her about Boston Pops conductor Arthur Fiedler missing the reception in his honor because he had persuaded my dad to drive him downtown to the scene of a fire. He was an honorary fireman in Boston and never missed a fire.

In high school I emceed a radio panel program of teenagers for the YWCA on political topics including the bigotry of Joe McCarthy; wrote a column on the visiting artists for the symphony program and ran the switchboard; cashiered and sold hats at my dad's store. The temptation to eavesdrop at the switchboard was great; I sweated over making change, and I loved trying on hats between customers. Eventually, during summers in college, I wrote obituaries and proofread for the only newspaper in town. My proofreading career almost ended before it began when I missed an obvious misspelling in a banner headline.

Given that background, it never occurred to me that men and women weren't equal—equally smart, equally able to earn a living, equally influential.

Both my father and my mother assumed I would go to college, have a career of some sort and marry. While I had many insecurities as a child—about my looks, my popularity, my acceptance by the "in" set, I was secure in their love, assumed civic participation was what everyone did, and never wondered whether my gender would render me a second-class citizen. I hoped I would marry—that was the measure of success for a woman of my era. I did not doubt that I would have a career—in what I had no idea, although government and political science captivated me, and writing came more or less naturally.

Four years at Smith College solidified that confidence. It opened a world to me where intellectual curiosity and being a study nerd were the norm. Although the socially popular girls abandoned the campus on the weekends for dates at the men's colleges, women ruled in the classroom during the week. There was no inhibition about asking questions and using our brains. Because I was a poor test taker but a competent writer, I entered the honors program that finessed tests in favor of papers and a thesis.

I was blessed with an advisor, John Chapman, who was both scholar and pragmatist. He arranged for me to work in the city planner's office in New Haven, Connecticut, for a semester as the basis for my senior thesis on city planning. New Haven was a city whose mayor had made planning the cornerstone of his administration. At a time when I was tiring of the purely scholarly life, Mr. Chapman rekindled my interest in researching the theory behind the politics I watched playing out in New Haven.

After college graduation I went back to Corpus Christi to wait for my by-then fiancé, Michael, to be through with medical school and internship—his condition for getting married. I was hired full time by the *Corpus Christi Caller-Times*, this time as a reporter for the Women's Section.

I loved being a reporter. It made use of my liberal arts education and enabled me to write—even if the editor spent the first year telling me that I always put the lead to my stories in the last paragraph. It gave me a chance to meet all sorts of people: the mother who, despite her young son's deafness, was determined to raise him to cope with a normal hearing world; the seniors living in the rural areas around the city who had come to Nueces County in horses and carriages; the woman who made antebellum tissue paper dresses for dolls. In the course of the interview about the dolls, she talked of her childhood in Nazi Germany. She was taught from an early age in school to hate Jews, a hatred, she told me apologetically, that she could not erase. She did not know I was Jewish.

Michael and I were married in August 1962, and I moved to Houston where he was beginning his surgical residency at Baylor College of Medicine. There was never any question that I would continue working. Finances aside, I never gave it a thought since writing was what I did, just like surgery was what Michael did. Michael has always supported my professional and volunteer life and taken pride in it and me. He is the consummate partner and best friend.

I was able to set up interviews for one morning at both the *Houston Chronicle* and the *Houston Post*. My first interview was at the *Chronicle* with the managing editor (second in command). He cared only that my husband had a residency with *the* Dr. Michael DeBakey. He also told me the only job open was on the agricultural desk. What I did not know about agriculture would fill books. However, he told me to come back that afternoon to meet with the editor himself, Mr.

Steven. In the interim, later that morning, I interviewed with the editor of the *Houston Post*, who was very gracious and kind. I received a job offer. I held off saying yes and drove back to the *Chronicle* for the interview with its numero uno, Mr. Steven. He connected; he asked me about me. In the end he told me that if one found a good reporter, one made room for that person whether there was an opening or not. He wanted me on the paper. I instinctively knew he would be the reporter's editor and friend that he proved to be over and over.

Remarkably, between the time I met with the managing editor in the morning and Bill Steven in the afternoon, one of the reporters for the women's section at the *Chronicle* tendered her resignation. Mr. Steven offered me that job. I wanted to work for him, and the job was perfect. I said yes. The salary, while lower, was not enough lower to outweigh the chemistry. Although Michael questioned why I accepted a reporting job at a newspaper that paid slightly less than a job offer at the competing paper, I never regretted my choice.

Once again, I was writing—and winning awards for my writing. My byline was recognized. And I was learning, always learning: about how department stores are laid out to attract buyers, about the struggles faced by families with mentally retarded children, about teenage marriages, interior design, living with cancer. I interviewed the president of Smith College, famous authors, the wife of the British consul general, who was gentle and genteel and had a romantic English accent.

But Michael was chafing in a residency that was long on scut work and short on hands-on surgical teaching. About a year and a half after our marriage, he had had it. With my total support, he moved from a surgical residency in Houston to a surgical residency in New York, where he had interned.

I was daunted. The city was huge; the job market was tight; the competition was fierce; apartment rents were enormously high; everything we looked at was old and dirty. I was having no success until Bill Steven from the *Chronicle* stepped in. He called his old friend, the editor of *Look Magazine*, and at last I found a job—with the *Insider's Newsletter,* a political and economic commentary published by Cowles Communications, the publishers of *Look*.

My colleagues included women and men who subsequently became prominent political and economic reporters and commentators on the national scene—Jane Bryant Quinn and Cokie Roberts to name two. Jane was divorced with a young child but dating a handsome Air Force Reserve pilot, David Quinn; Cokie, the youngest of us, was newly married to *New York Times* reporter Steven Roberts. We three meshed well. Cokie, whose dad was the venerable Congressman Hale Boggs from Louisiana, would regale us with insider political stories. Her enthusiasm and energy were contagious. Jane was the sophisticate and most worldly. I'm not sure what role I played in the trio, but I loved being part of it. Michael and I were the witnesses at Jane and David's wedding. The reception planned for the Officers' Club after the small ceremony fell through. With nowhere to go, but wanting to celebrate, we packed up the wedding cake and headed for our tiny apartment with her parents (her dad being the high ranking officer of a major corporation) in tow. There, despite my mother's most earnest teachings, I had left the bed visibly unmade. I've rarely done that since.

The *Newsletter* was housed on Madison Avenue. One bank of windows overlooked the side of St. Patrick's Cathedral and provided a front row view of a Pope's visit. A one-block walk took us to the high fashion shops of Fifth Avenue. My subway ride each morning began at the foot of the George Washington Bridge and ended at Rockefeller Center. I loved walking among its mélange of underground shops, flower boxes that changed with the seasons, and, in December, admiring the giant Christmas tree hovering over the ice skating rink.

Our small staff interviewed cabinet members, Wall Street hotshots, inventors, headline makers. Our mission was to relay to our subscribers the latest news on the political, economic, scientific, and sociological fronts in succinct paragraph form. Our lawyers watched Harvard football games in boxes that bordered that of the Kennedy family. We heard all the most titillating gossip Washington and New York had to offer. Those who live in New York tend to think that little of importance in the world happens outside the five boroughs—and maybe Washington, D.C. While I didn't fully share that view, I was influenced by it.

I never wanted to rear children in New York because I thought children needed green grass and freedom to roam and a slower pace.

Their parents needed enough money to be able to avoid the awfulness of the subway crush at rush hour and grimy public school buildings and shootings in the garages under their apartment buildings. Nor was New York Michael's cup of tea, although he made the best of it and thrived in his residency.

But in my late twenties and childless, I loved New York's vibrancy, its diversity, its urgency and energy, its sense of being in the forefront of life. Once a week, unless Michael was on call, he would pick me up after the *Newsletter* was put to bed, and we celebrated with dinner at a cozy Irish pub. With friends, we treated ourselves to dinners at posh restaurants, trying a new spot each time. We reveled in second night openings of *Fiddler on the Roof* and *Man of La Mancha*.

Our apartment was in a middle-class housing project that rose at the base of the George Washington Bridge. The soot and noise from the cars passing under our building were the bane of my housekeeping, but the view of the fireworks up and down the Hudson on the Fourth of July made it worthwhile. We took our laundry to the little Chinese laundry man across the street until he was beaten up by the Mafia. We bought our worms from the corner fishing shop that received its supplies from the same Mafia. We fished off the beach at Montauk. We strolled through the grounds of The Cloisters and spent weekends with my aunt and uncle at their tree-shaded house in Englewood, New Jersey. It was there I recovered from the death of our first child hours after she was born.

Those were years of exhilaration and joy and exuberance and learning one another and solidifying a marriage. They were years of figuring out how to share and partner and have patience. They were years of making friends together and dreaming of a family. Years of sorrow and tears that taught us what was important in life and that blueprints do not always work out but that what Michael and I had separately and together was very, very good.

And through it all, for both of us, was our work, fulfilling and expanding and a part of who and what we each were.

Then Michael finished his residency and made ready to undertake his commitment to the Berry Plan. He was committed to a two-year stint in the Air Force as a captain. The transition about which I'm writing was beginning.

I began to grapple with an inner struggle that forty years later rises

146

again as I contemplate retirement: a nagging sense that I was losing who I was, a slow rediscovery of who I really am, and a tug of war that to this day still marks my life. For all the achievements of the women's movement through which I lived, we have not yet figured out how to easily juggle wifedom and motherhood, a career outside the home and managing the home. It is a high-wire balancing act that is tough to achieve and hard to live through.

But back to the transition. I was about seven and a half months into my second pregnancy. We were trying not to be apprehensive but not totally succeeding. Neither were our families. Michael's father was a doctor, and his parents wanted me to come to Corpus Christi for the birth so Dad could oversee my care. We agreed I would do so after Michael completed basic training.

We landed in Wichita Falls in January—winter grim, gray, and unfamiliar. Michael was gone each day learning how to be military (something he never quite achieved). I spent the day in our motel room doing needlework on an altar scarf for my mother-in-law who was about to become the head of her Eastern Star chapter. Adjustment number one. But it was temporary, and Michael and I were together. Motherhood and wifehood were paramount.

Basic training completed, Michael went off to Amarillo. I went off to Corpus Christi, where, in due time, our first son was safely delivered under his grandfather's eagle eye and the obstetrician's steady hand. Michael was there for the birth, but returned to Amarillo shortly thereafter. I spent a week with my parents and a week with his, and then, tiny infant in carrier, I flew off to our new home.

I cannot say the days became routine. But they certainly were a transition.

Office dress was traded for burp cloths and Texas casual.

Conversation about the politics of the day was traded for tips on what to do about colic.

Shopping was done at the PX—a brightly lit '60s version of Costco. Only basics; forget fashion—unless khaki and black dress shoes are your thing. Forget Fifth Avenue. I am sure Amarillo had lovely stores but the Air Force base, which was in the process of being closed, was forty miles from town.

Instead of opening nights on Broadway, we amused ourselves with horseback rides in Palo Duro Canyon, which, by the way, we loved.

We were not experienced riders but we plodded slowly through the brush with the canyon walls on either side of us and imagined the early settlers in their isolated cabins and the last of the Indians appearing on the horizon.

At a luncheon for medical wives, the commander's wife thanked one of my friends for her lovely "quickie"—it was, indeed, a very delicious quiche.

The chaff from wheat harvested the previous fall lay in drifts against our back door instead of sooty snow on the sidewalks. Prairie dust covered the window sills instead of carbon dirt from the exhaust of cars on the Cross Bronx Expressway, which ran below our New York apartment building. While the chaff reminded me, pleasantly, of one of my favorite childhood books, *Little House on the Prairie*, I perversely yearned for the soot and the noise.

The crowning blow came when the ABC network laid off Dick Cavett, an egghead talk-show host—my only real link to the so-called worldly conversations of my urban days. I wrote an anguished letter of protest to the powers that were. It obviously fell on deaf ears.

The saving grace was two of our "class" of medical wives—all of us new to the service and none of us "career military": an artist whose imaginatively themed weekend cookouts added zest to our off time and a new bride from the East Coast whose husband had reported to duty barefoot and in shorts.

Baby Louis grew and thrived in Amarillo but before he was a year old, we were on our way again, our belongings and baby packed into the car. Our destination was the Upper Peninsula of Michigan. I had no idea of what we were in for, but I was very, very grateful that Michael was not headed to Vietnam. We knew from newspapers and television and from our career military friends that the war in Vietnam was hell, that one could not tell friend from foe, that death and injury were just beyond the next footfall. And we knew about the long, fearful waits of the spouses left on the base to hold down the domestic fort.

Again our move was made in the middle of winter. Louis had a raging fever by the time we reached Chicago, and frantically we had to consult doctor-granddaddy by long distance. When we arrived at K. I. Sawyer Air Force Base, we were greeted by twenty-one feet of snow. It was not sooty but it was high. We walked through a snow canyon which rose above our heads to get to our temporary home—a trailer at the end of a runway where SAC bombers kept their engines running all night so they would not freeze.

This time Michael was the head medical officer. We soon moved into a duplex on the base. By now I had adjusted to motherhood, acquired some confidence in my ability to love and care for this wonderful child for whom we had longed. But I still missed the other part of myself. The endless struggle to keep the house neat and clean, cooking meals, and opening cans of Spaghetios, Vienna Sausage, and Le Seur baby peas (which were all Louis liked to eat) did not quite fill all the space that my writing and paid job outside the home had occupied. A piece of me was missing.

So began my volunteer life.

I volunteered to write the Officers' Wives Club newsletter—anything to do a little writing again.

I volunteered with the Red Cross, learning to take pulses (sort of) at the hospital. We took in one of the children of a pilot's family when they had a family crisis.

We watched Louis rock on his rocking horse and learn to walk.

And we were very grateful to be together, Louis, Michael and I. Better cold in Michigan than hot in Vietnam. It came close to us. Our neighbors and fellow residents on the base were pilots who flew supplies and relief missions to the war theater. We knew how blessed we were. Family was far away, but we had each other.

We kept eighteen-month-old Louis awake to watch man's first step on the moon.

We went to the woods to cut down our own Christmas tree. We learned to shop in the Sears catalog and waited with bated breath for the spring and holiday editions. Our big day out was to drive the miles and miles into town to the Kmart that had just opened.

Michael learned to ice fish and trap with a male nurse anesthetist.

The month of summer in August was glorious. Wildflowers covered the meadows. The sun shone, but the breeze was cool. Butterflies flitted, the sky was astringently blue, and the clouds were stereotypically puffy.

Then, halfway through our second winter in Michigan, our tour of duty was over. Michael accepted a job with a surgeon in Houston. We flew down and bought a house over one weekend. The movers packed up our belongings, and once again, we settled ourselves into our car.

We headed into yet another transition. A transition that eventually, some years down the road, took me back to a job outside the home, this time in government rather than journalism.

However, in the interim my sense of loss of self became greater. I loved being wife to Michael and mother to Louis and, not too long after we arrived in Houston, our beloved Noah (also born under his grandfather's watchful eye). But where and what was the kernel that was the essence of me?

I was Michael's wife and Louis's and Noah's mother—both of which I definitely wanted to be and could not survive not being. But I also needed a piece that was purely and simply me.

In between carpools, I tried my hand at writing children's stories with minimal success (déjà vu, my mother's rejection slips). I joined the League of Women Voters, ultimately moving onto the national stage to head up the organization's ERA effort in 1979. In the course of organizing our campaign, I met President Carter and shook his hand just outside the Oval Office—what a thrill! We lost the fight to amend the Constitution but we took another step forward in women's battle for equal opportunity. Noah played in his playpen, permanently installed at the League office in my early years there. Later he would plead with me to come home from my board trips to Washington. I did. The ERA was important; motherhood was more important. I PTO'd and served my congregation and other community organizations as a volunteer. The boys tolerated with great patience the fact that Mom was always late picking them up from school.

The loss subsided but never quite went away. I do not know why. Again, I loved rearing my boys and being Michael's wife. I earned recognition with my volunteer work. I think I made a little difference in my own small corner of the community. I even managed, eventually, to sell a couple of children's stories to *Humpty Dumpty Magazine*. My life and my inner person were enriched by each new challenge.

But for whatever reason, the loss was there in the background until, in the late '70s, when both boys were well ensconced in school, I went back to work part-time at a paying job outside the home. The journalist husband of a journalist friend from my *Chronicle* days asked me to take over the direction of Election Central. This was a vote-gathering and counting service organized by Houston's two major newspapers and three network television stations. It was a unique bridge from my outside-the-home professional life as a journalist to my outside-the-home professional life in government.

It is interesting. After my mother and dad closed the mom-and-pop music store they owned and operated for twenty-five years beginning when I was in college, my mother tried to return to the volunteer world. It did not satisfy her. "I don't feel as though I matter," she told me, "if I'm not earning money for what I do." She went back to work part-time in a bookstore at age seventy. Being paid made her feel worthwhile and valued in a way volunteering did not. Maybe that was it for me, too. Certainly the worth of my writing was validated by being paid for it as have been my many years in government. But I do adamantly consider managing a home and rearing children and being a volunteer to be professional work and basic to life. I have never given up the volunteer work or the mothering or the wifing. The first six months I volunteered as a Senior Council Aide were no less valuable than the remaining twenty-nine and a half years I have spent on salary in government work.

Through all the transitions, I have ultimately discovered who I am. The kernel was right there in front of me all along. It is what we all discover. I am not one thing. I am many. I am a government wonk, a writer (infrequently now), a wife, mother, grandmother, volunteer, needlepointer, reader, friend. No one piece is more important than the other but it takes all of them to make a whole. When one of those pieces fell away all those years ago, I lost a piece of myself.

The tug of war remains. The seesaw still tilts from side to side. I still feel guilty when my husband sits home alone at night while now, in my seventy-third year, I cope with the challenges of a new job, a new transition. I still feel guilty when I cannot get to Dallas or Austin as often as I would like to be with the children and grandchildren because my job is demanding. Even though I know who I am now, the fear of loss nags once more in the back of my head—will I again lose me when I do finally retire in the not very distant future and give up the outside-the-home, paid professional piece of my life?

Although the thought nags, I hope not. There is a time and a season for everything, and I have long since proven myself to myself in both my journalistic and government careers. It is getting to be time to let go of that piece. But all these years later I still remember when I left journalism and the strident energy of New York to become, at least temporarily, a full-time wife and mother.

However, there is another difference now, too. These days I know without the slightest doubt that my greatest joy and my proudest moments are not the stimulating and creative time spent as a journalist in Texas and on Madison Avenue or the wonderful volunteer boards on which I have served or the great satisfaction of public service at City Hall, as much as they are part and parcel of my essence and always will be.

As I look back on all my many transitions, my greatest joys and my proudest moments all involve my very beloved husband and friend, my cherished sons and their dear wives, and my treasured grandchildren. They are the fruits of my transitions, the blood of my heart. All the rest is just icing on the cake.

And so, when I retire, it will be fine. I will be me. I think.

The Midnight Visitor

Thelma Zirkelbach

With Ralph

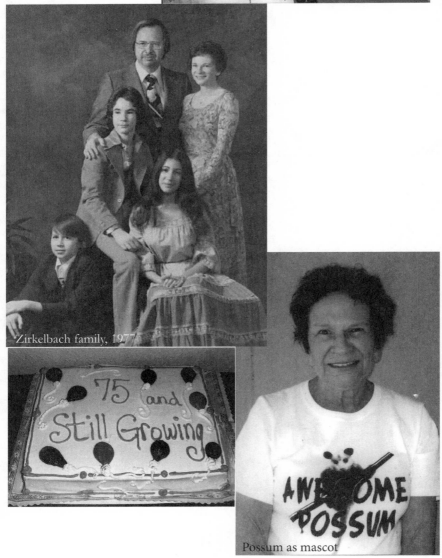
Zirkelbach family, 1977

75 and
Still Growing

AWESOME POSSUM

Possum as mascot

The Midnight Visitor

Thelma Zirkelbach

I am a member of a club I never aspired to join: The Society of the Recently Widowed.

I never wanted to go it alone. I'm a team player, a tandem rider. I had a roommate after college, a partner in my business, and two husbands—at different times, of course.

Widowhood puts me in good company. In every species, from humans to chimpanzees, chickens and even fruit flies, females outlive males. I thought I had outsmarted biology by falling in love with and marrying a man five years younger than me. I hadn't counted on cancer robbing me of my spouse. But what seemed like an annoying sore throat was the first symptom of acute myelogenous leukemia, an insidious disease that claimed my husband's life in less than a year.

Widow. I hate that word. Months before my husband died, I pictured myself as a widow, a dried-up, sad old lady with lips turned down and shoulders hunched. That's the connotation of many widow synonyms—dowager, beldam, crone, hag. Even matron sounds unflattering. Most of all, widow means alone.

My husband, Ralph, was the center of my life, my best friend and confidante. Even when he was hospitalized, in and out the first few months, and continuously the last seven months of his life, he talked me through every problem, every decision.

In August 2005 his doctor told us the disease, which had been in remission, had resurfaced. There were no more options. After a stunned silence, Ralph said, "I'd like to talk to Dr. Craddock alone."

Trailed by my son and daughter, I made my way to the family lounge, sat down at the table, and began to sob. When we began this cancer journey, we'd had such hope. Now we'd heard a death sentence.

A woman ambled into the room, opened the refrigerator and turned to stare at me. She stood still, holding a cup and watching me.

Hadn't she seen anyone cry before? Especially here, in a cancer hospital? Finally, I couldn't stand her scrutiny any longer. I jumped up and snarled, "Get out of here." When she scuttled out of the room, I slammed the door behind her.

"Mom!" my son gasped. "This is a public place."

"I don't care," I wailed. I continued weeping until the nurse called us back to Ralph's room. Then I pulled myself together. I would not cry again in public.

My tears wiped away, I opened Ralph's door and met his eyes. As if he'd lowered a mask over his face, his expression was blank.

"Do you have any questions?" the doctor asked me.

I had dozens: How much time? What can we do? Why did this relapse happen? But all I could say was, "Will Ralph still get dialysis and other treatments?"

Ralph glanced at the IV bag that connected to a catheter sewed into his chest. Because he couldn't swallow, he also had a feeding tube through which he got nourishment. He had a rectal tube, a urinary catheter, an oxygen cannula. I'd become used to all the tubes, but sometimes when I looked at them—really looked—my heart hurt. My robust, active husband now resembled a concentration camp victim, seventy-five pounds lighter than when he entered the hospital, with sticklike limbs and only wisps of hair.

"As far as I'm concerned, the treatment can stop," he said.

Was that what he had told Dr. Craddock? Would a nurse come in and disconnect the IV, pull the catheter out of his chest? "Let's think about it first," I pleaded.

He sighed. "All right."

The doctor left and the children followed. I reached for Ralph's hand. It already felt cold, or perhaps I was only imagining it.

He didn't tell me what he'd said to the doctor and somehow I couldn't ask. We spent the remainder of the weekend in silence and sorrow.

Despite what he'd told the doctor that first awful day, Ralph wasn't quite ready to die. During the next weeks the machines stayed on.

His family came for a final, bittersweet visit. He held his mother's hand, joked with his sisters. They laughed about the time he'd connected the telephone to a loudspeaker and broadcast his sister Karen's conversation with her boyfriend through the house. They reminisced about the summer the kids thought they'd unearthed an Indian burial ground and dug up the backyard searching for bones, then endured their father's anger when he discovered what they'd done.

While they talked, Ralph's mother sat quietly, her eyes full of tears. After the visit she would never see her oldest son again. Except at his funeral. I wiped away my own tears. My heart hurt for her, for all of us.

As the days passed, I grabbed each moment and hung onto it. I wanted to believe the doctor had made a mistake, that Ralph would survive, the leukemia would disappear. But his strength was ebbing, he spoke less, he seemed more passive. He'd been the dominant partner in our marriage, always in charge. Now I'd have to take charge of my own life, become more self-reliant. In the words of my favorite song, Ralph had always been "the wind beneath my wings." How would I fly without him?

"I don't want you to leave me," I told him one day, laying my head on his bed.

He stroked my hair. "You'll be all right. You'll do something good."

I hoped so. Meanwhile, I planned his funeral in Iowa and a memorial service afterward in Houston. I gathered papers I would need, visited with the banker for Ralph's business, and in an impulsive rush of proactivity, baked a cake to serve after the memorial and put it in the freezer. As days went by and Ralph grew weaker, I began cleaning out his hospital room. I didn't think I could handle that—afterward.

I made myself a promise: I would not let widowhood define me. There is a Yiddish proverb that says, *Az me muz, ken men*. When one must, one can. I vowed to make that my creed.

On Friday, October 14, Ralph's doctor took me aside and said gently, "It won't be much longer, maybe twenty-four hours."

Shock took over. My emotions shut down. I didn't feel a thing; yet I was compelled to count each hour that Ralph still lived. Twenty-four, twenty-five, twenty-six. Perhaps the doctor was wrong.

Ralph's brother called. Ralph was too weak to lift the receiver so I held it against his ear. When I put it down, he clasped my hand. "I— love—you," he murmured. Those were his last words to me.

Sunday morning I sat by the bed, patting his arm. The nurse came in to check the monitors and I moved out of the way and turned to glance out the window when I heard her soft gasp. "He's stopped breathing," she said.

I swung around. He looked the same. Wasn't his chest moving? Wasn't that his sigh I heard—or was it mine? The room blurred through my tears. The nurse put her arm around me. "You should call your children."

I thought I was prepared, but no one is really prepared for a loved one's end. Death isn't real until it happens. Even then, you can't believe you'll never have another conversation, another argument, another hug.

The children came, stood numb and quiet beside the bed for a while and then went into the hallway, leaving me alone. I kissed Ralph's forehead, then trudged out of the room. *Our* life was over; *my* life had begun.

The first months were filled with the myriad emotionally-draining tasks that follow a death—probate, Social Security and insurance claims, bank account changes, car title changes, will change, beneficiary changes—each of which took far more time than I anticipated. I felt as if I were on a roller coaster, one day bursting into tears at the bank, another yelling at the postal clerk who sent me home to get papers to prove I could change Ralph's post office box to my name, another evening sobbing uncontrollably when I turned on the television and happened on a program Ralph and I used to watch together.

I worried about household emergencies. That had been Ralph's domain. My grandson Marco knew full well how inept I was. His first question after Ralph died was, "What will Thelma do when something in the house breaks down?"

Cry.

Things did break down and I did cry. My water heater developed a gas leak; my hard drive crashed, taking a nearly completed manuscript with it; my air-conditioning unit needed a major overhaul; one stormy morning my roof began to leak. That time I didn't just cry, I howled. Even everyday chores were harder to manage without Ralph's presence—moving heavy boxes, retrieving something from a high shelf, fastening a necklace. During my first months of widowhood, I survived a fall in the middle of the night. I drove myself to the emergen-

158

cy room—carpal tunnel surgery, a hysterectomy. I spent special days alone—New Year's Eve, Ralph's birthday, Valentine's Day—mourning for the one person who'd always been at my side.

I joined a grief group soon after Ralph died and found support and solace in the company of others who had loved and lost. One evening the group leader told us that we were blessed to have loved someone enough to mourn them. His statement turned grief on its head. How tragic it must be not to have someone to grieve.

Along with the pain of parting, I remembered happy days with Ralph: good and sometimes not so good-natured political debates, listening to *A Prairie Home Companion* as we drove along a highway, sharing Thanksgiving with our children and their children, walking along a beach in Cozumel just before dawn. I remembered one night glancing at the TV after I'd removed my glasses, noticing a blur of pink and remarking, "Look at those dancing girls."

"Put your glasses back on," Ralph said.

"Oh, my gosh." Not dancing girls, but flamingos. Several days later two garish, pink plaster flamingos appeared in our backyard. Even for Ralph, the gaudy birds were too tacky for the front lawn.

As the months passed and the first waves of grief subsided, I began to gain confidence. I put together a support system for household emergencies, financial advice, and computer glitches. I even found a good-natured handyman for minor repairs. I refurbished our "junk room," cleaned out Ralph's files, invited friends for dinner, planned a vacation with my sister.

But my singular life-changing experience occurred on Labor Day weekend, nearly a year after Ralph's death. On Friday night I awoke to the sound of breaking glass. I assumed the cats had engaged in one of their nightly wrestling matches and had knocked something down. I got out of bed to scold them. To my surprise, Toby, cat number one, was in the living room, dozing on Ralph's chair. I opened the door between my bedroom and the combination bathroom-dressing room and found Tiki. But as I glanced in, I noticed her tail swishing wildly as she stared at the counter. I followed her gaze and spied something gray. Another cat?

I grabbed Tiki, shut the door, shooed her away, and then peeked in again. Sitting on my counter, staring placidly at me was the most enormous possum I'd ever seen. We eyed each other like members of two rival gangs: the Jets and the Possums.

What to do? Certainly not go in and confront the menacing marsupial, not with its sharp teeth. Try to chase it out into the garden? Same problem. I slammed the door.

I wanted Ralph here. Right then. But I reminded myself that he wouldn't have been any more able to deal with a wild animal than I was, and with that thought I got back in bed and went to sleep.

Near morning I woke and began calling the SPCA, the Humane Society, every place I could think of. A holiday weekend was the worst possible time to get help. Finally I located a private company. By the time they arrived, the possum had disappeared. "I'm not crazy," I told the two young men who stood in my bathroom, looking perplexed. "I know there's a possum in here."

"Don't worry. We'll find him."

Now that help had come, I was worried for the possum. "What will you do to him?"

"Let him go in the woods."

They searched and found my guest. He must have climbed down from the counter and ambled from the bathroom to the dressing room and into my closet where he was hiding in a shopping bag. He'd entered the house through an opening in the attic, pushed down the attic stairs and made himself at home. I had the house animal-proofed several days later.

Soon after the animal control people left, a friend called. "You sound tired," she remarked.

"I am," I admitted. "I had an overnight visitor."

"Oh my," she said. "I didn't know you were dating."

"Well, I had a male guest, but he was a possum."

"All night? Weren't you scared?"

"No," I answered. "After I found him, I went back to sleep."

"You're a tough lady."

Me? I hadn't considered that. But she was right. I'd handled the possum episode with aplomb. No pounding hysterically on my neighbor's door or phoning my children in the middle of the night. Of the two of us, the possum was probably more alarmed by the encounter.

I don't know how he felt afterward, but for me our stare down worked wonders for my self-esteem.

Now I felt brave enough to face anything. Well, not a bear or the slopes of Everest, but strong enough for situations I might reasonably expect to encounter. Thanks to that midnight visit, I have become a more self-actualized person, confident that I can meet whatever life tosses at me.

Of course, I haven't stopped missing Ralph. I always will. But I've found a new synonym for widow: survivor.

In Search of Georgio

The Hunt for George Clooney and Other
Revelations along Italy's Lake Como

Montage by Lisa Hankamer

Lisa Hankamer

In Search of Georgio

Lisa Hankamer

Europe, Lake Como, Italy— August 2004

It is our last day in Lago di Como and we have the strongest desire to make it something truly spectacular. We need to create a lasting impression for what has truly been a fun and free-spirited vacation in this jewel of a town. Bellagio, located in the heart of Lake Como, has been a wonderful discovery. It was serendipitous that my friend, Mary, and I were able to coordinate a visit to this lovely Italian peninsula at the same time. But, I digress.

This is our last day. The lovely couple from Australia, who for a week had been inhabiting the room next to mine, and with whom Mary and I had become balcony mates every evening at cocktail hour, inform us that they have reservations for lunch at Villa d'Este. This bastion of old-world elegance is world renowned, one of those truly upper-crust establishments, where only the rich and famous grace its reservations system at a minimum of $2,000 per night. Mary and I decide that lunch at Villa d'Este is just the type of finale we deserve for topping off our travel adventure.

So, after a quick breakfast of chocolate croissants and hot tea, we approached the front desk of our hotel (Hotel Belvedere), in order to make lunch reservations. "I am sorry, luncheon at Villa d'Este is not possible today," explained the concierge, "an emergency economic summit has been called. Berlusconi is right now holding meetings with the former prime minister of Israel. The entire hotel has been shut down to outside visitors."

Of course, this news does not dampen our spirits. We had dressed the part today. We are ready to have some fun, and we look really hot for "women of a certain age." We view "certain age" as only a minor setback, and we set out. On the walk down to the ferry (or water taxi if you prefer—everything around Lake Como revolves around the water transport schedules), Mary makes the most wonderful gesture to me, the gift of a silk scarf—something to add a little panache to the black number that I am wearing. Further, she has received instructions on how to tie the thing in the European manner and she now utilizes her newfound expertise on me. We are ready, willing, and able for anything that comes our way this day.

A little history is required at this point. I had chosen to spend this week discovering Bellagio while my husband would be happily engaged in a highly demanding, eight-day trek around the Monte Rosa, the second highest mountain in the Alps. He was part of a Swiss tour group that was backpacking (with all of their clothes and toiletries on their backs) up into the Alps, hiking over nine hours each day, and spending each night in cute, albeit rustic, *refuges*. I had been a participant of this naturalistic pursuit two years before, with an eight-day, mule-escorted trek around Mont Blanc. Although truly an awesome experience, this time 'round I was searching for a little more relaxation and fewer smelly socks. So, my husband and I parted company in Zermatt; he to the Alps—and me on my five-day mission to discover the northern Italian Lakes and Bellagio.

This departure from being the Traveling Couple to flying solo would be new to me. At the time, I didn't realize just how closely this departure was foreshadowing my future. However, as my bus careened around the narrow twists and turns of the lake road towards Bellagio, I promised myself that should I arrive alive, first purchase would be an enormous rosary or a shitload of prayer beads. Then it hit me. I was actually traveling internationally. All alone. To an unknown place.

In the past, in my role as my husband's traveling partner, I had received the benefit of his fluency in four languages and the ease with which he moved amongst different countries and cultures. I had also been imprinted with his abhorrence of being labeled as one of those "Ugly Americans." Complicating my current situation further was the fact that the "Idiot from Texas" (as they referred to him here) currently had his cowboy boots propped up on the desk in the Oval Office. Fearful of committing a major international faux pas, I vowed then and there to maintain a low profile during this sojourn. I was determined to fit in and to be immersed in the rhythm of the local culture. And yes, I would even attempt to communicate in the local language. The fact remained that here I was at my age, worried over the impression that might be left with people whom I would most probably never encounter again. Perhaps this was all simply a protection tactic on my part, but I was damned if I wouldn't keep them guessing at my port of call.

My associate and coworker, Mary, heard that I was taking off on my own during my upcoming European trip and couldn't resist the opportunity to throw caution to the wind. She would travel to Bellagio and keep me company for the five days that I was scheduled to be there alone. Things at our office had been pretty tough for some time. The commercial real estate business had just not been fun for either of us lately. Mary had reached that mental nirvana of, "It's now or never, Babe," and this trip was offering an immediate solution—*escape*! Secretly, I think that she was also yearning for a chance encounter with a local Italian Stallion.

Hey, if she wanted to join up, it was up to her. I was leaving for Switzerland the next day and was unable to help her with arrangements. So, I provided her with my dates for arrival and departure in Bellagio, the name of the hotel where I was staying; suggested that she might want to fly direct into Milan and take the train to Lake Como; mentioned the necessity of taking a ferry to Bellagio; and wished her luck. I gave her a fifty-fifty chance of showing.

Fast forward. After parting from my husband and six train changes, a bus, and then a ferry later, I finally arrived at the Hotel Belvedere in Bellagio with my first priority being to order a large bottle of Prosecco as a welcoming gesture for Mary's expected two o'clock arrival. After I savored three flutes of Italy's famous sparkling wine, I concluded that Mary was a no-show and a siesta was in order. At 7:30 p.m. I received the call, "I'm here! Let's go get something to eat!"

Upon finishing a second bottle of Prosecco and consuming a wonderful dinner of *pescada grilliata*, Mary shared her travel story with me. She had been enjoying an uneventful flight up until the moment she realized that she had left all of her travel information— hotel name and address, etc., along with all of my careful instructions, back in the States. She made the decision to literally fly by the seat of her pants and obtain directions from all Italians that she encountered. Did I mention that she had no cell phone with her? She didn't. She did have the foresight, however, to hire a professional clothes organizer prior to leaving, who helped her shop and pack for the trip before she left. This girl has her priorities.

I learned that the first Samaritans she encountered were an elderly Italian couple who helped her board the right train at the Milano Malpensa Airport. Another gentleman at the train station escorted her to the ferry landing upon her arrival in Como. Two traveling Americans on the boat, who were brothers, thankfully prevented her from getting off at the wrong stop. Mary had also chosen, by mistake, the nondirect water taxi which took her on the complete, four-hour tour of the lake before finally landing at Bellagio. Luckily, the brothers were headed to Bellagio as well. The stress of her trek, though probably daunting to most humans, was completely invigorating to Mary as she was making new friends at every turn. Amazing!

For the next five days, we explored every nook and cranny of the Bellagio peninsula. No bistro or pizza parlor was passed up and we found plenty of excuses for Prosecco stops. There were gifts to buy for friends back home and a visit to the thermal spa was part of our agenda. We even accomplished a four-hour hike up one of the subtle mountains surrounding the lake. And, par for the course, Mary befriended a German-speaking couple hiking the same path. Our encounter resulted in a shared picnic complete with photo ops. We also became close to the wedding party from Oregon that was ensconced in the hotel our same week. They didn't seem to mind at all when we crashed their wedding party, dancing the night away under the stars.

On the night prior to our last day, there was finally time for quiet reflection. While sitting on my balcony in full awe of an amazing sunset, I came to realize the different approaches Mary and I were exhibiting toward new environments. My inclination was to be low key, attempting to meld into the local culture. Being fearful of doing something incorrect, I attempted to pretend that I was one of the locals, abhorrent of calling attention to myself. I even felt compelled to try to communicate with the locals in their own language as a gesture of sincerity.

Mary, however, showed no such inclinations. She met no strangers. She was speaking to everyone she met—in English! And, overnight, she had mastered the Italian art form of gesturing; utilizing every one of her limbs to get her point across. And not surprisingly, she disarmed one and all. Her exuberance was contagious. Little by little, wherever we happened to be walking in the town, we were hailed with cries of, Hello Mary!" "Buon giorno, Mary!" People were waving from the rooftops of hotels (the two American brothers) and all the shopkeepers knew her by name and were genuinely happy to see her. Mary conquered the town of Bellagio within her first twenty-four hours and I was simply dumbfounded.

This trip was already so much more meaningful to me than I could ever have expected, as I had learned something very important. It really doesn't matter what country you are traveling, people will usually respond positively to a positive spirit, regardless of what language that spirit is speaking. Mary's uninhibited approach taught me how much more full the Journey is when you are not worried about being proper, are not concerned with what others are thinking of you, and not obsessed with fear of mortal embarrassment. I realized that I had been operating for some time in accordance with others' views of How I Should Be. My "Aha" moment set me free to go forth, to love and embrace all of this human spirit that is Me. I could not have picked a better launching pad than Bellagio.

So, today is our final day in Italy. We dash onto the ferry with all of our enthusiasm for adventure unfolding. Upon disembarking, we board a smoking bus that would take us up to the next town where Villa d'Este is located. Mary engages the diminutive Vietnamese lady sitting across from us in gold-flecked flip-flops into conversation. She finds out that the woman is also going to Villa d'Este. Mary inquires how long she would be staying there. While rolling her eyes, this woman, a cleaning employee, replies that she works at the hotel. At any rate, she provides us with directions for walking the last thousand yards to the hotel once we get off of at the bus stop.

We immediately run into a precious Welsh couple—whom Mary had conquered and befriended during our stay. They have just been turned away from the Villa d'Este gates. We quietly determine that it might have been their attire of Bermuda shorts, Birkenstocks, and the husband's Sherlock Holmes chapeau that may have had some impact on the lack of welcome they had received. We determine to persevere, and at least have a good look at the place.

Upon cresting the hill, we see it there before us, the beautiful, grand entrance to Villa d'Este. Oddly, we notice the entrance is lined with about five hundred Italian soldiers in full regalia, accompanied by their machine guns. With Mary tagging behind, I walk up to the only hotel employee visible who is manning the gate. "Reservations," say I, "for Hankamer?" The young lad smiles and opens the gate for us. Mary and I, to our astonishment, are allowed to enter and thereupon begin walking through the beautifully sun-dappled entrance toward the hotel. Mary still seems to be lagging behind, even as I regale her with the beauty of the day and the various flora and fauna of the gardens and the absolute splendor of Villa d'Este. I choose to ignore the soldiers lined up and down the entire drive. I sense that if we act as if we belong, no one will know the difference. Mary is still behind me and very silent. First time in days.

As we stroll around to the entrance, there are several military vehicles parked in front with even more soldiers packed inside. We enter the hotel. Total mayhem is in progress. Agents with crew cuts and earphones in every visible orifice are swarming the hotel lobby. Mary is still quietly following me as I wind my way towards what I hope is the restaurant. A young waiter greets us. "Reservations," I say, "for Hankamer?" Of course, I *know* that I am asking *permission* for a reservation. So far, however, everyone seems to think that I already have a reservation. This is the true beauty of miscommunication. The young waiter asks us if we wish to be seated inside or out on the terrace next to the lake. I turn to Mary, who appears to be shell-shocked at this point, then I turn back and request terrace seating, with a lakeside view.

Once seated, I order a little Prosecco for us. We've had quite an experience thus far and I, for one, am parched. Mary is still silent and stricken. I ask her what is wrong. She gushes forth that since we entered the gates, she has been extremely petrified that we were about to be arrested. She was expecting to be shot at every moment. This is the first time during this trip that she is actually tongue-tied, overwhelmed by images of herself in an Italian jail. The reality hits her that she still has no cell phone, and no way of calling anyone to our rescue. I have to admit, I relish the situation and the opportunity to knock her off her feet. She is sincerely terrified. We will have to address her fear of authority with a professional upon our return to the States.

We settle in to a sinfully delicious three-hour lunch on the terrace with only two or three other tables being served. The maître d' regales us with stories about huge waves coming over the bulkhead of the terrace and wiping out the entire dining experiences of the guests—along with hairpieces and fake eyelashes. There were once hammocks hanging out over the water, which some needy diners used to appropriate after a long afternoon of dining. For us, the exciting part is watching the agents swarming back and forth. There are Navy SEALS (or whatever their Italian counterparts are), swimming along the bulkhead checking for, can you believe it—— bombs! We also observe several naval marine vessels on the lake patrolling and taking video shots of those of us eating. To this day, we have no idea where our photos might have landed.

Giddy on bubbly, we decide to take a walk in the magnificent gardens. The day is still young and I become inspired. I remember that George Clooney's house is purported to be located in a small village not far from this hotel. Actually, a waitress in one of the bars in Zermatt was from this town called Laglio, and indicated that George spent quite a deal of time there when not filming. George's film with Julia Roberts, *Ocean's Twelve*, has just finished shooting. So, the impromptu decision is made: Mary just has to have a George Clooney encounter before we return to the States. Thus begins our search for Georgio.

Unfortunately, our bus transportation is not scheduled to arrive for another forty-five minutes. Frightened of losing our buzz (and courage) we decide to take off on foot in the direction of Laglio, Georgio's village. Now, the road is quite narrow and winding around Lake Como. It also begins to turn quite hilly on us. As we traverse the side of the highway in our high heels, we begin passing through police barricades. We just smile and act as if this is a normal afternoon stroll. There also seem to be a lot of police cars going back and forth, with the occasional military helicopter hovering over us from time to time. Fifteen minutes into our climb the thrill of adventure is beginning to wear off. I comment to Mary that with all of these police swarming back and forth, wouldn't it be nice if one stopped and gave us a ride? She visibly shudders at this point.

At that moment, a policia car pulls over. I immediately pull out my map and point to Laglio. Mary in halting Spanish (couldn't believe she wasn't speaking English) asks them how far to Laglio. We determine it is another fifteen minutes via car. We are desolate. Explaining to the carabinieri that our feet are very tired and, pointing to our muscled calves, we emphasize that we must get to Laglio in order to meet Georgio Clooney. Surprisingly, they load us into their car for the ride. Fifteen minutes later, we are best of friends with Rodolfo, Sergio and Alonzo, who evidently moonlight as band members in the evening hours, and have invited us to a concert to watch them play the next evening. Unfortunately, we will be traveling back. In true camaraderie and upon exchanging many cheek kisses and taking photos, they let us off in the heart of the town. Laglio. Actually, it is only two buildings coming together at a very narrow spot in the road. Our "chauffeurs" call out to a local villager who has stepped out of his shop to inspect our group, "Filipo!" He's to become our caretaker now. He speaks English as his former wife was French and they lived in Scotland for twenty years (all this in about two seconds of conversation) and he will take over now. The policia limousine is actually out of its jurisdiction and the group is in a hurry to get back to the town of Como. We wave goodbye and place ourselves in Filipo's hands.

Filipo, in his mid-sixties I would guess, immediately charms us with his welcome. He points out Georgio's house and informs us that he left only the day before, headed to Cannes and what a shame, as he had been spending quite a deal of time there since completing the film. By now, Filipo's friend, Jean Piero, has joined us and we enter Filipo's domain—the Laglio tobacco shop. We meet his eighty-six-year-old mother, who is helping him to mind the shop along with his cat, Pisspot, who is prominently perched on the counter.

Filipo informs us that we will have to purchase a bus ticket in order to get back to the water taxi launch for transportation back to Bellagio. What luck! The tickets can be purchased from Filipo's shop. However, the bus will not be arriving for another forty-five minutes. So, Filipo invites us to the Laglio bar, next door, for a drink. Jean Piero follows and a few other locals who have heard all the commotion, join us as we enter the bar. Thereupon, the merriment begins. Filipo, an excellent host, orders a magnum of Prosecco. The noise level rises as we all attempt to communicate with one another, sharing bits and pieces of our lives. Music is wafting through from some unknown source. Jean Piero, we are told, has an excellent wine cellar. Alas, if only we had more time. Enrique is portrayed as a ladies' man; Mary is warned not to look into his eyes or she will get pregnant.

There is a frail artist in the corner drawing our pictures. Filipo orders another magnum of Prosecco. Mary is suddenly dancing the tango out into the street with Enrique. Filipo has to excuse himself every five minutes to run next door and make sure Mamma is okay with running the store. In between political discussions not favorable to George W., we are being taught cork tricks by another inebriated patron. More locals have entered the bar. It's packed and pandemonium reigns. We are introduced to the gentleman who sold Georgio his villa. He promptly pulls out a photo of himself and Georgio shaking hands at the closing. Mary returns, flushed from all of her street dancing, and suddenly it's time to get on the bus. With a flourish of grandeur, Filipo escorts us to our coach as we wave goodbyes to our newfound friends. Upon providing detailed instructions to the driver, a relative of course, Filipo graciously kisses us goodbye on both cheeks and our bus pulls away.

For the fifteen minute ride to our ferry launch, Mary and I are both speechless. Not until we board the ferry and are headed across Lago di Como to Bellagio with the wind in our hair do we dare speak. What an incredible day we have just experienced. We could not have choreographed a more meaningful and memorable lasting impression of this idyllic place. In searching for Georgio, we have found so very much more. The spirit of Northern Italy, the engaging warmth of the people living in the area, and even our own devil-may-care sense of adventure took us totally by surprise. We end this last night on a quiet note. A light dinner— pasta and salad— and a glass of Prosecco raised to the richness of the experiences that we have encountered that day and the new friendships that have been made along the way.

Epilogue

I returned to Lago di Como two years later with my husband. I had so wanted him to appreciate the place that had become a watershed for me, creating such fond memories. We pulled the car over in Laglio and I asked a strolling local of Filipo's whereabouts, as his mother no longer appeared to be tending the shop. Suddenly, Filipo emerged from the bar and we commenced to having an uncomfortable kind of reconnecting. I don't know why. Perhaps it was my husband's presence? Perhaps too much time had passed; too many things had happened; life's changes had taken their toll. Who knows? I had one last hug and one last photograph was taken of the two of us together. And then, I simply smiled, waved farewell. I continued the Journey with the newfound realization that I, myself, had helped to create the vibrant experience of that trip. And that I was perfectly competent and capable of creating the same kind of wonder and enlightenment in my life every day. I soon chose to continue pursuit of the Journey on my own. My husband and I parted company in a friendly manner and I now live in a state of wonderment as each new adventure unfolds.

See and
Be Seen

Illustration by Barnet Levinson photo by A. Falk Jepson, 1964

Susan Briggs Wright

The little granny and Snow White

Briggs girls, 1951

From the *Stanford Quad*, 1965

Producer/Anchor *On The Record*, Houston Public Television, c. 1985

See and Be Seen

Susan Briggs Wright

"Talk only about the thing which interests you for the moment," Mark Twain wrote in his posthumous autobiography, "Drop it the moment its interest threatens to pale, and turn your talk upon the new and more interesting thing that has intruded itself into your mind meantime."

I wasn't sure where this story might take me when it intruded itself, but I knew exactly where to begin. I remember the scene so vividly that it could be happening right now.

It is the summer of 1960 and I am at Benson Optical in Minneapolis. I have been eagerly anticipating this occasion for years. At seventeen, I am finally about to get contacts! I believe that the glasses I am wearing are thicker than any the optician will see in a given year. The convex lenses magnify my eyes, but whenever I move my head, my eyes are obscured with light reflections and distortion. In profile, I look like my vision is blocked by opaque white disks. So I am absolutely dumbfounded when the optician asks me, "Are you sure you really want to get contacts?"

"What does he want me to do," I growl to myself, "throw my glasses on the floor and jump up and down on them?"

Having worn glasses since I was eighteen months old, I was very sure that I really wanted contacts. I quickly adjusted to the foreign objects in my eyes and began a milestone transition. What would my life have been like without contacts? Very different in a thousand little ways, and at least one big way—I could never have been a television journalist wearing those glasses, not even in Whitehall, Wisconsin, the small town where I was born. Shortly after my TV debut in Houston, the news director suggested that I get green contacts to hide the fact that I have one blue eye and one light brown eye. The station had gotten calls about this distracting feature. I made the change, and the station publicist planted a tongue-in-cheek newspaper item about viewers thinking there was something wrong with their TVs.

My eyes have been a lifelong topic for discussion. A serious issue emerged one day while I was being fed in my high chair. The spoon was loaded and, as my eyes began to focus, my left eye headed for a spot next to my nose. My parents wasted no time taking me to the eye doctor. He said I had a condition called lazy eye, caused by a weak muscle that could be surgically tightened when I got older.

I was given tiny glasses that fit my face, but if they helped me see better, why didn't I keep them on? Instead, the glasses would frequently disappear, be recovered, and put back on my face. One day my glasses couldn't be found at all. "Where are your glasses, Susie?" "Gone to New York, Mommy," was the cheerful reply. I had flushed them down the toilet! My sister Barbara, who was about seven, clearly recalls the plumber's visit. I don't know what ideas I had about New York, but my feelings toward the glasses were obviously negative. After that, a little black cord kept them on. I am certain that I spent my first three and a half years in a blur.

We moved to Eau Claire, where someone told my parents about Dr. Walter H. Fink, a Minneapolis ophthalmologist who specialized in my type of problem. I liked him; he exuded competence with his impeccable grooming, kindly face, and calm voice. His dictum was that I was extremely farsighted, with a lot of astigmatism to boot. Surgery wouldn't help; I needed better glasses. My own vague memory of the new glasses is that they felt heavy. But as my parents told it, when we got home, I jumped out of the car and pointed to the house across the street. "Look, Mommy," I said, "that house is made of bricks!" Mother started to cry.

Dr. Fink was delighted with my next exam, telling my parents, "I've opened up a whole new world for this little girl." It was true. The new glasses stayed on. Some of my earliest memories are of sitting alone under the piano with books. I loved the transformations—raggedy Cinderella turning into a princess with the wave of a wand—and a turn of the page. I gazed at Snow White and fantasized that magic could turn my white dandelion-fluff hair to the shade of a raven's wing.

The school year had already started when Mother walked me into Miss Marian's busy kindergarten at the state teachers' college campus school. Miss Marian played three notes on the piano, summoning the children to meet me. I looked them over as they sat cross-legged on the floor and spotted a girl with white skin and shiny black hair. Just like Snow White! After Miss Marion introduced me, I went right over to Snow White and sat down. I didn't get the welcome I wanted. She greeted me with a bubbly laugh saying, "You look like a little granny with your white hair and glasses."

I was taken aback, but somehow able to recognize truth telling without malice. I loved school and before long, a few flashy acrobatic tricks dispelled the granny image. Snow White became a good friend and we still communicate despite the miles and years. But I had been put on notice. I had an impediment to overcome in this new world. Even today, I cringe when I hear someone described as cross-eyed. But my misbehaving left eye was apparent to other kids only when I was swimming. At school, I was more likely to be called "Four Eyes" or "Googly Eyes." That didn't happen often, but at home, I would complain to my parents that I was ugly. Daddy gave me a mantra straight from his heart, "Don't worry about that. Just be Susie Briggs."

I became highly attuned to the labels grown-ups attached to Susie Briggs: precocious, willful, stubborn, imaginative, a real live wire, a handful, and, as Grandpa Joel put it, "not like Barbara" which clearly meant "not well-behaved." Barbara, four and a half years older, has always been a sunny presence in my life. When people said she was mature, smart, responsible, and a real little lady, I was more proud than jealous. But I was quite jealous of my peers who were fawned over because they were beautiful, darling, pretty, and/or cute. Even when I received compliments, I would imagine or perceive a silent qualification: *Too bad about those glasses.*

In second grade, I liked being seen as the little bookworm standing on a library chair to reach the fifth and sixth grade shelves. At first, I had to read aloud from my selections before I could check them out. One summer day in Grandma Millie's attic, I found *Anne of Green Gables.* I was instantly enamored with Anne's elegant vocabulary and with Anne herself who, like me, was not a beautiful child. Anne was taunted about her impediment, which happened to be her red braids. *Carrots!* I was happy to learn in sequels that Anne's tresses turned to rich auburn. I loved the world of books. It was a reliable visual environment that became my comfort zone. I also sensed that reading sharpened my wits, and helped me attract the friendly attention I craved.

Recently, to remind me that I wasn't the only one wearing glasses, Barbara mailed me some old snapshots showing both of us in Whitehall wearing our spectacles from the small-town eye doctor. Coincidentally, and out of the blue, Snow White sent me a Briggs Christmas card from 1951. Fourteen-year-old Barbara, holding baby Dorothy would soon discard her glasses; she outgrew her farsightedness. Toddler Mary Alice was six months away from getting convex lenses, not quite as thick as mine. I painfully witnessed occasions when adults cooed adoringly over Dorothy's big blue eyes, and in the next breath, bemoaned the fact that "poor Mary Alice," who was very much present, had to wear *those glasses*. I had no hope of outgrowing my vision problems. But not long after that Christmas, Dr. Fink told me that doctors were developing tiny lenses to rest right on the surface of my eyeballs. When I got older, I could wear glasses that would be almost invisible. I could hardly believe it, but it gave me hope.

There were times when my glasses made *me* invisible. In junior high, I tried out for the lead in a school play, but realized the teacher in charge was paying absolutely no attention to my reading. I'm happy to say that I bear no scars. Whatever I missed in the genetic lottery for vision equipment, I more than recouped by landing in the egalitarian culture of Eau Claire during the fifties. In junior high, the kids who put out the school paper created the ideal girl and boy by identifying individuals with the best eyes, figure, smile, and hair (Snow White's category). I was surprised and amused to discover they had managed to include me: Ears—Sue Briggs. My thick glasses didn't prevent me from having two very nice steady boyfriends. I was happily active with cheerleading, tumbling, band, the school paper, and whatever was happening with my large clique of girlfriends.

The long-awaited scene at Benson Optical came just before my senior year. I was ready for the thrill of a dramatic transformation. But Dr. Fink limited my contact lens wearing during the first year. I spent school days in glasses, but savored evenings and weekends, discovering peripheral vision and the wide-open feeling of my naked face. Before contacts, when an acquaintance would ask me to take off my glasses—the better to see my different-colored eyes—I worked hard to avoid focusing, aided by my silent chant, "Left eye, left eye—don't you dare turn in!" But now I no longer worried about looking cross-eyed. I could swim (carefully) wearing my contacts. About the time I was excitedly splurging on eye-liner, mascara, eyebrow pencil, and five colors of eye shadow, I read a *Life* magazine feature on the cosmetic industry, "delirious" over the explosive growth in eye makeup. A Revlon executive said, "If eyes hit Minneapolis, kid, they're here to stay." I was pleased to do my part from Eau Claire.

Our senior class play was a Roaring Twenties musical. I showed up bespectacled after school to practice the Charleston and the Varsity Drag. On dress rehearsal night, I wore my fringed chemise, my contact lenses, false eyelashes, and, of course, eye makeup. I noticed the drama teacher watching me dance, for the very first time. With undisguised amazement, he said, "Wow! You've really got it!" I recall it as a "duckling to swan" moment that was tinged with cynicism. I saw how easily Sue the swan could gain advantages. But how unfair to Sue, the duckling! While smiling at the drama teacher, I was thinking, "You phony. I'm the same dancer you've been ignoring all this time!"

Without a barricade of bulging glass, people were more likely to notice my unusual irises. I began to enjoy these inspections, sometimes feigning shock, "What? Two different colors? They were both blue this morning." In situations where I was accustomed to matter-of-fact treatment (*Men seldom make passes at girls who wear glasses*), I now felt an extra little sizzle. I no longer had to do or say anything special to earn attention. (*Girls who are pretty don't have to be witty*). But I felt strangely ambivalent about compliments, and was often ungraceful in responding.

Mother wondered why I had two senior class photos made; one with glasses and the other with contacts. I explained that some friends might prefer the glasses version because that's how they had most often seen me. Now, as a memoir writer, I see someone who hadn't liked being the girl with thick glasses, but wasn't ready to leave her behind. Maybe I wanted to honor the fact that I had earned a safe place in my little world while wearing them. "So," a friend said after reading my first draft, "I'd love to see your senior picture in your yearbook. Did you use the version with glasses?" Well, no, of course not.

The transition to contacts was a satisfying flourish to cap off my school years in Eau Claire. It seems odd that some low marks in physics and lackluster performance in chemistry and geometry didn't mar my image as a high achiever. Our high school counselor summarized my tests with complacency. "You're intelligent, but not well-rounded. High on verbal and analytical skills and low in areas related to math and geometry. You don't roll very well," he chuckled. "And you probably won't become an engineer." The message I bought into was that girls could kiss off math and science.

In college, I ditched English for a psychology major which allowed a lot of creative writing and outlier courses such as "Theater of the Absurd," one of my favorites. The psych major also required statistics, which I nearly flunked, but my other grades were good. I was bound for a real career—something creative and glamorous, like publishing, journalism, or advertising. For my rarely worn glasses, I chose eccentric black diamond-shaped frames, with the fuzzy notion that weird specs would telegraph self-confidence and a sense of fun. One guy I dated briefly got a surprise when I showed up wearing the glasses. "Wow!" he said. "Just like coke bottle bottoms!" Thick glasses—the perfect acid test for second dates. I had never liked clothes that were too frilly or cute, but now I consciously aspired to be elegant. The Palo Alto photographer who did my engagement portrait suggested his favorite approach for blondes: a casual pose, wearing white, against a white background. "No," I told him, "I'm not a California girl."

A recent breakfast in the garden: I pose a question to my husband of forty-six years, "Darling, do you remember the first time you saw me wearing my glasses?" "No." "Well, suppose I had been wearing my glasses at Stanford the day you spotted me. Would you have taken the trouble to find out my name?" "Probably." Decades of journalism kick in and I follow up, "That's really interesting. How many girls did you ever date who wore glasses?" "I never paid attention," he says wickedly. "When things get serious, the glasses come off anyway."

These days, my thoughts center on what's behind my eyes, a whole new world of the right brain and its links to vision. I wonder what development should have been going on in that hemisphere during the fog of my early years. I have always avoided brain teasers, puzzles, and many tasks that involve working my eyes and hands together. From childhood, I found these activities disagreeable, especially compared to the easy rewards of reading or the fun of practicing cartwheels. Would an early grasp of space and proportion have made it easier to enjoy math and science? If my vision had been corrected earlier, might I have done better in statistics? I find myself watching a toddler in the dentist's waiting room. She happily focuses on slapping a puzzle together. Admiring her speed and confidence brings on a strange, wistful feeling that I quickly dismiss.

Back in high school, I accepted the common wisdom that my strengths and weaknesses had been set in place at the factory. In college I learned there were critical periods of development with deadlines for acquiring various capabilities. But these fatalistic assumptions have been upended. "One word—" says the neuroscientist to graduates of a certain age, "neuroplasticity!" The latest strategy in the battle against Father Time is to stimulate our brains so that they will form new links and work around areas of weakness. Neuroplasticity: use it or lose it.

Following Twain's advice, I am dropping the questions about my early vision issues; interest has indeed begun to pale. I am on notice that however vision-deprived I was as a helpless infant, looking forward is more rewarding than looking back. The newer and more interesting thing that is now intruding itself is the realization that I am empowered (goaded) to get busy and improve my brain by focusing on those areas I always tuned out. I transpose my parents to the twenty-first century, "Quit whining about physics. You're starting with a tutor on Tuesday." Instead of sitting here in my comfort zone, writing, I should be working on Sudoku. No pain, no gain.

I've tried Sudoku. Twice. Now the flashbacks take me to a scene in fourth grade. I'm in pain over long division. Miss Mesang has kept me in from recess. She thinks I'm goofing off and is taking a firm hand. She stands over me and my paper, which is full of black marks and erasures. "Susan Briggs, you are smart enough to do this." "But I *can't*!" I cry out in frustration. In retrospect, I see that wretched paper and many others like it. I can never seem to keep columns straight. I make mistakes filling out forms, writing the response for Line A on Line B. In fact, I have just made a long list of weaknesses that I see as "allergies," some have been career-limiting: In addition to statistics, there is Microsoft Excel, financial documents, graphs and charts, and using my eyes to figure how anything mechanical really works. Not only have I accepted these allergies, I've come to cherish some of them, as if they were virtues. "I hated piano because I had trouble reading music, but my (mean) parents made me keep taking lessons." "My dear, our wedding vows did not address road maps. I don't do road maps!" I've nurtured the art of avoidance behavior to such a high level that I could teach it as a master class.

I am wearing my glasses as I type this. On the rare occasions when I wear them in public, I experience some of that invisible feeling older women complain about. I think back to the time I got something in my eye that scratched the cornea. It was just before my thirty-fifth high school reunion. My then-optometrist said, "Maybe it's time to take away the contacts." I shot him a murderous glare. But at the reunion, enjoying friends I hadn't seen for years, I didn't feel the dreaded transformation from swan back to duck. I recognize that my eyes are the oldest part of me and when they've been worked hard, they are uncomfortable with the contact lenses. I fear and loathe any prospect of giving up my contacts, even though I know that seeing is more important than being seen.

Once upon a time, my story would have been a fairy tale. A cross-eyed toddler muddling around in a foggy world finds a kindly wizard who enables her to see. In her seventeenth summer, she is suddenly made pretty by new and improved magic. Transformations make good fairy tales. Transitions are what we experience in real life. There are transitions ahead that won't be as much fun as getting contact lenses. Or as minor as a possible return to glasses. Old age means big changes—losses—to manage through. For now, I will focus on neuroplasticity: Attack the allergies, be leery of the comfort zones, stay alert to the downside of self-acceptance, and make sure I am challenged every day. But I can still pass a mirror in my glasses, smile at the little granny Snow White saw, and gratefully recall Daddy's mantra.

Acknowledgements

The first person for me to thank is Suzanne Kerr. She introduced me to The Transition Network and was my first sounding board as I considered leading a special interest project on memoir. This wasn't an organization of professional writers—which was one thing that particularly interested me. But would we find women ready to commit to publication, provide comments and suggestions to other members, and meet deadlines? "TTN women can be counted on to deliver," she said, and proceeded to back me up in each and every step of our transition from idea to book.

This group did deliver—thoughtful questions and insights, camaraderie, enthusiasm, and good stories. In working with visual elements and other matters between writing and printing, we gained much from the skills of Mary Margaret Hansen, Donna Siegel, Jane Williams, Sandra Wotiz, Thelma Zirkelbach, and Hope Fonte. Susan Lieberman's leadership of our TTN chapter and her supportive participation have been significant assets to this project. Tremendous encouragement has also come from The Transition Network's national office which provides a continuing framework for its members around the country to discover new connections, resources, and opportunities. The website is www.thetransitionnetwork.org.

Our manuscript benefitted greatly from the expert line editing and advice provided by Susan Hayes. Any sins against Chicago Style are errors or hard-headedness on our part.

Virginia Houk at Texas Review Press brought our vision to these pages with layout and design. Barnet Levinson of Barnet Levinson Design created the cover illustration with a photograph by Laurie Perez.

We are all especially grateful to Dr. Paul Ruffin of Sam Houston State University, publisher of Texas Review Press and 2009 Texas State Poet Laureate for making this book happen.